Living Through History

THE SPANISH ARMADA

DAVID McDOWALL

B.T. Batsford Ltd London

Typeset by Tek-Art Ltd, West Wickham, Kent
Printed in Great Britain by
R J Acford Ltd,
Chichester, Sussex
for the publishers
B.T. Batsford Ltd
4 Fitzhardinge Street
London W1H 0AH

ISBN 0 7134 5671 X

ACKNOWLEDGMENTS

The Author and Publishers would like to thank the
following for permission to reproduce
illustrations: J. Allan Cash for figures 10 and 51;
BBC Hulton Picture Library for figures 7, 38, 41,
46, 47 and 58; Bodleian Library, Oxford, for
figures 15 (Wood C.43 p.130), 45 (Mason Q233T)
and 60 (Wood C.43 p.78); The British Library for
figure 33 (MS Cotton Augustus I i 38); The British
Museum for figures 1, 4, 5, 20 (MS 48027) and 21
(MS 48027); Mary Evans Picture Library for
figures 3, 14, 36 and 44; Foto Mas for figure 32;
Master and Fellows, Magdelene College,
Cambridge, for figures 23 and 24; Mandel Archive
for figures 17, 19, 25, 27, 29, 30, 31, 34, 35, 37, 42,
52, 54 and 56; Mansell Collection for figures 6, 11,
12, 13, 39, 43, 49 and 50; Museo Naval, Madrid,
for figures 8, 28 and 40; National Maritime
Museum for figure 22; National Portrait Gallery
for figures 9 and 16; George Philip and Son Ltd for
figure 53; Ulster Museum for figure 57; Victoria
and Albert Museum for figure 59. Figure 2 was
drawn by R.F. Brien; Figures 18 and 48 were
taken from Garrett Mattingly, *The Defeat of the
Spanish Armada*, Jonathan Cape, 1959. Figure 26
was taken from Peter Padfield, *Tides of Empire*,
Routledge and Kegan Paul, 1979. Figures 53
(© George Philip and Son Ltd) and 55 were taken
from Niall Fallon, *The Armada in Ireland*, Stanford
Maritime, 1978. The pictures were researched by
Patricia Mandel.

Frontispiece
"Royal Game" by Reynolds (*Tate Gallery*)

Cover Illustrations
The colour photograph shows a section from
"Armada Tapestry" (*National Maritime Museum*);
the portrait is of the Duke of Parma (*Mancell
Collection*); the engraving shows the battle of
Portland Bill (*Mandel Archive*).

CONTENTS

THE ILLUSTRATIONS

THE GATHERING STORM

On 30 May 1588 the largest fleet ever assembled – consisting of 130 ships, 20,000 soldiers and 10,000 mariners – sailed from Lisbon. Its purpose was to assist the Spanish army in the Netherlands to cross the Channel and invade England.

The fundamental reason for the Armada lay in the rise of Protestantism, which destroyed the old fabric of European relationships and brought new groupings of political interests. This did not happen overnight, and Philip II of Spain tolerated 20 years of provocation before he finally despatched the Armada against England. He had watched his commerce in the New World damaged, his citizens robbed and killed by English marauders and his ambassadors insulted. His reluctance to attack England lay in the complexity of European politics. He could not afford to drive Queen Elizabeth into the arms of France. In the 1560s he had hoped to marry her, and thus continue the Anglo-Spanish alliance sealed in his marriage to her half-sister, Mary Tudor. But Elizabeth had refused to say either yes or no to Philip's proposal and had stuck to her Protestantism. It was this which had persuaded the Pope in 1570 to denounce her as a heretic and encourage the Catholic powers to overthrow her. By 1571 Philip seemed keen to do so: "I am so attached to it in my heart, and am so convinced that God our Saviour must embrace it as his own cause, that I cannot be dissuaded."

In fact, Philip could very easily be dissuaded, and the greatest discouragement lay with France, Spain's main rival for European supremacy. While France remained strongly Catholic and Elizabeth remained on the English throne, there was little danger of a robust Anglo-French alliance. But Elizabeth was childless, and her heir apparent was Mary Stuart, since 1568 under house-arrest in England. Mary was half French, so Philip saw no virtue in removing Elizabeth only to put Mary on the English throne.

In 1562 France had entered a long period of crisis, as Catholics and Protestants fought for

1 A Protestant allegorical picture. The ship – marked at the masthead with the Chi-Rho, the symbol of Christ, and the hull "Europe" being steered safely to port by Protestantism's "helmswoman", Elizabeth, and crewed by Burghley, Walsingham, and Leicester.

2 Map of Europe in 1580, showing the extent of the Spanish empire.

control of the country. The struggle had been further complicated by dynastic problems. By the 1580s the French King, Catholic Henry III, wanted to reconcile the Catholic and Protestant factions, because he faced problems on both sides. The heir apparent, Henry of Navarre, was also leader of the Protestants. It was unlikely that French Catholics would accept a Protestant king. On the other hand, Henry III feared even more the Catholic League, who were also fighting the Protestants, and the League's leader, the Duc de Guise.

One reason for this fear was that Philip II had chosen to support the Catholic League in order to weaken Henry III's position. He wanted France to remain divided so that Spain could continue to dominate the European political scene. More particularly, he wished France to be so fraught internally that she would be unable to make trouble in the Netherlands, where she had territorial claims. Philip had an even stronger reason to support the Catholic League. If the Protestant Henry of Navarre defeated the Catholics Philip would face the prospect of a Protestant coalition led by England and including France, his rebellious Dutch subjects, and the Lutherans of Germany. In such a situation Spain's authority and power would be severely threatened.

Suddenly, after 30 years of hesitation, Philip had to act decisively to ward off the various dangers. He nurtured the Guises, to neutralize Henry III and to use their kinship to Mary Stuart to wean her away from hope of rescue by France and encourage her in attempts to overthrow Elizabeth with Spanish help. These plots, of course, eventually brought Mary to the block, but, in the meantime, she had been induced, by Philip's skilful machinations, to disinherit her son, James VI of Scotland, and bequeath her claim to the English crown to Philip.

Philip also had to persuade Pope Sixtus V of the validity of his claim, and instructed his clever ambassador, Enrique de Olivares to remind his Holiness,

I cannot undertake a war in England for the purpose merely of placing upon that throne a young heretic like the King of Scotland, who, indeed, is by his heresy incapacitated to succeed.

After Mary's execution the need of Papal recognition became more urgent, partly because Armada plans were well under way, but also because Philip feared that the pro-French cardinals might arrange James VI's conversion to the True Faith. After Mary's execution Olivares had asked the Pope for financial support to overthrow Elizabeth. He cleverly used the Pope's anxiety to avoid pledging money to extract the Pope's promise "to agree with whatever his Majesty thinks best in the matter [i.e. Mary's successor], and he will do what may be necessary". Four months later Olivares took things further:

With regard to the question of the successor, his Majesty assumes that his Holiness will already have been informed of the well-known fact that when the Queen of Scotland was taken a will was found, in which she left his Majesty [Philip] heir to the crown. . .

In July, Olivares triumphantly secured official Church recognition that "Your Majesty might appoint the Prince or Infanta" as sovereign of England. He also managed to bully the Pope

into making the pro-Spanish Catholic exile William Allen (see page 66) a Cardinal.

Philip had been driven to weave this skilful web not only by factors in the Catholic world, but because of growing provocation from England. There had been two prevailing points of view amongst English foreign policy-makers. One was pragmatic: to pursue diplomacy and avoid confrontations. But the other, led by Walsingham and Leicester, urged open hostility to Spain, based partly on the expectation that the Huguenots would prevail in France. Before long, this party was giving unofficial support to the French Huguenots, and to Philip's Dutch Protestant rebels in the Netherlands. As the danger of provoking Spain became more apparent, the peace party tried in vain to pull England's foreign policy back to the more neutralist line of the 1560s. But, as a result of Catholic plots, popular anti-Catholic feeling ran high. Mary Stuart's execution was in part a sop to that feeling, even though it also threatened to antagonize, and even unite, Spain and France against Elizabeth.

Amongst the provocations of the more Protestant-minded were the privateering

3 Pope Sixtus V (1585-90), who reluctantly recognized Philip's claim to the English Crown, but avoided paying towards Elizabeth's overthrow.

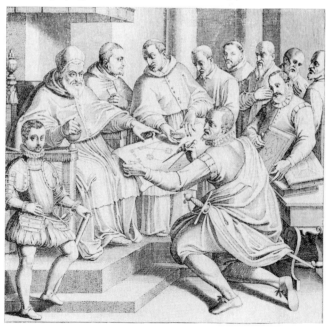

MarieR

5 Mary Queen of Scots, aged 30, as she appeared on a medal in 1572.

4 Elizabeth I, aged 55, as she appeared on an Armada commemorative medal.

voyages to the New World, which they financed, and which they persuaded the Queen herself to finance. These trips, like Drake's voyage around the world (1577–80), were extremely damaging to Spain. More serious, however, were England's relations with the (since 1556 Spanish) Netherlands. Most of England's trade had flowed through the Netherlands for centuries. The Dutch revolt stemmed from Philip's unwillingness to tolerate Protestantism and his decision to break with past practice by ruling without allowing local nobles the kind of say in affairs which they had enjoyed in the past. These nobles were more aware than Philip that the Protestant merchants played a major part in making the Netherlands the centre of North European trade. Philip's repressive policy was damaging their economic as well as their political interests. In 1568 recalcitrance turned to outright revolt, which Spain found impossible to stamp out completely, in spite of savage military campaigns.

England was caught in a conflict of interests. She wished to continue her trade, and recognized that Philip was the lawful overlord of the Netherlands. On the other hand, she did not wish to see the Protestant rebels defeated, since they were potential allies if Europe found itself plunged into a war between Catholics and Protestants. For some time England tried to continue her trade and also give quiet, unofficial assistance to the Dutch. But by helping the rebels England's position was eventually clear, as was Philip's. Dutch ships used English ports to sustain the rebel-held coastal areas of Holland and Zealand, and English volunteers went to fight for the rebels. Elizabeth tried to keep the level of assistance sufficiently half-hearted so as not to provoke a Spanish reaction.

In the mid-1580s, however, the situation started to deteriorate rapidly. In 1584 the Dutch leader, William of Orange, was assassinated, leaving the rebels in quarrelsome disarray and leaving Elizabeth as the only Protestant leader of substance standing in the way of Spanish hegemony. A year later, the Spanish recaptured Antwerp, the commercial capital of the Netherlands. Unless help came, the Dutch revolt looked like collapsing within a year or two. For England the danger was twofold: Spain was unlikely to allow English trade back through its territories and, more importantly, it was almost bound to attempt the overthrow of Elizabeth once it was so strongly placed across the Straits.

Consequently, the war party successfully urged Elizabeth to conclude an alliance with the Dutch and to send an army, under the Earl of Leicester, to help them. This army achieved very little, but its despatch was tantamount to an open declaration of war. Meanwhile, Drake was sent on an openly warlike expedition westwards, sacking Vigo before sailing to the Caribbean, where he proceeded to plunder and sack some of Spain's richest ports. Throughout 1586 not a single Spanish silver ship crossed the Atlantic, and Philip's bankers were beside themselves with anxiety.

The despatch of Leicester's expedition pursuaded Philip that until he controlled the Channel the Dutch rebels would not be crushed, and that only by the conquest of England could the Channel be controlled. In 1586 Philip began the feverish military preparations to make conquest possible.

6 In 1573 Spanish troops sacked Harlem, massacring all the Dutch inhabitants. Even in an age used to slaughter, Protestant Europe was horrified. It was also highly counterproductive, since it hardened Dutch opposition to Philip.

7 "The King of Spain's Navy is Abroad", a romantic Victorian view of Elizabeth with her counsellors, discussing how to meet the Spanish threat.

THE PLANNERS

In any great undertaking, human nature plays its part. Whether or not the invasion of England was feasible was not merely a matter of the military power Spain could muster, but the way in which this power could be deployed. Philip required absolute obedience in his servants, and that meant that he required absolute control. He studied the various plans meticulously, and he was probably correct in his conclusion that a direct sea-crossing from the Netherlands, twice suggested by Netherlands' commanders during the 1570s, was far too risky. He rejected a seaborne invasion solely from Spain because of the enormous cost involved, with no certainty of success. Such decisions were well within his grasp. What was beyond his control – and possibly beyond his understanding – was the human element – the need of his commanders to feel they were genuinely part of a team, rather than servants of his will. Ultimately, the Armada planning failed because Philip had no sensitivity for getting the best out of his subordinates. And, while he sat immured in the Escorial (his palace/monastery retreat), he was defeated by distance – from his general in the Netherlands, and from his admiral in Lisbon.

Alvaro de Bazan, Marquis of Santa Cruz (1526-88)

It was the Marquis of Santa Cruz who offered to invade and defeat England by seapower. In 1581 he had played the major part in the capture of the Portuguese fleet, acknowledged to be superior to the Spanish. The following year he heavily defeated a stronger French fleet off the Azores. In the mistaken belief that he had worsted English as well as French ships, he had made his offer to Philip.

Santa Cruz was a seaman to his fingertips, coming from a distinguished maritime family, and a noble one, too. His career had started early. At the age of 14 he was guarding the Straits of Gibraltar, and at 18 he defeated a superior French fleet in the Bay of Biscay. For 20 years, from 1561 to 1581, he was a tireless fighter against the Turkish threat, sustaining Spanish footholds on the North African coast against Turkish attack and raiding Muslim ports. And he was a veteran of the great sea victory over the Turks at Lepanto in 1571, a victory greater then any had dared hoped for: "It seems to us a dream, for never was such a naval victory heard of."

Lepanto was fought with galleys – fast, oar-powered ships, which were used to ram and board an adversary. Although galleons as well as galleys were present in the Azores the battle was decided by boarding. But such tactics were becoming obsolete, as English naval tactics were beginning to show. Walter Raleigh, himself a naval tactician, thought the French admiral, Peter Strozzi, deserved his defeat: "To clap ships together without consideration belongs rather to a madman than a man of war. For by such ignorant bravery was Peter Strossie lost at the Azores."

Santa Cruz set to work assembling and building ships for the Armada in January 1586. He proposed a fleet of 150 great ships

8 The Marquis of Santa Cruz.

and over 350 smaller vessels, requiring 30,000 mariners and 64,000 troops, at a cost of over one-third of Spain's annual revenue. Philip rejected so costly a venture and instructed him to build a smaller fleet, to be ready by summer 1587 and strong enough to hold the Straits of Dover and ferry the Flanders army across to England. One of Santa Cruz's juniors had already warned Philip not to underestimate the enemy:

The sea forces which the enemy can collect are very great and will increase daily, unless some strong effort be made to render Your Majesty's present small number of vessels more than equal to the multitude of the enemy. It is all very well to say that Your Majesty has a hundred galleys. They may be of some little use in the Mediterranean but they are of small importance elsewhere, especially on the High Seas.

Santa Cruz went on to tell the King what was required:

His Majesty should put together a fleet and should send it out to seek and fight the English. The galleons of His Majesty in Portugal, and those in the river of Seville, should be got ready, careening and caulking them so that they may be fit for any voyage, however long. Futher forty five great ships . . . must be refitted, armed, commissioned and victualled for eight months.

Such preparations could hardly be kept secret, and the English government knew very well

. . . that by information the King of Spain is preparing a great army by sea, part at Lisbon, other in Andalucia, and within the Straits [of Gibraltar], all of which was judged should meet at Lisbon and the same come for England or some part of Her Majesty's dominions.

So Drake sailed in late April, instructed by the Queen "to impeach [impede] the purpose of the Spanish fleet and stop their meeting at Lisbon". The means were left to his discretion, though he was "particularly directed to distress the ships within the havens themselves". In Cadiz harbour Drake sank Santa Cruz's flagship and 23 other large vessels. For Santa Cruz, bottled up in Lisbon and unable to give fight, it was a considerable embarrassment. Philip remarked, "The loss was not very great, but the daring was very great indeed." And the incident has gone down in history as "singeing the King of Spain's beard".

In fact, Drake's presence off Spain inhibited the Armada preparations for at least eight weeks, a crucial period, for by the time Santa Cruz was ready the equinoxial storms of autumn necessitated postponement of the expedition until the following year. Santa Cruz was aware of Philip's growing impatience and his failure to understand that one could not set sail, without the gravest risks, between October and April. Throughout the autumn and winter he was chivied with letters from Philip, demanding that he be ready to sail by December. By the standards of the day, Santa Cruz was already an old man, and he started to show the strain. He fell ill and died in February 1588, some said crushed by the reproaches he had received from Philip.

King Philip II (1527-98)

Nothing was as critical in the preparation of the Armada as the character of King Philip himself. He had been assiduously trained for kingship by his father, Charles V, and was destined for a life of seriousness and meticulous administration. Philip was 29 when his father abdicated the crown of Spain in 1556, but from that day he plunged himself completely into the affairs of state. He worked all day in his office, reading reports and writing instructions, to keep his enormous empire running. (The Spanish empire included the Netherlands, the duchy of Milan, the Kingdom of Naples and Sicily, the Caribbean and much of the seaboard of Central and South America, and, in the Far East, the Philippines.) Philip resented interruptions to his deskwork and tried to fend off all but the most necessary interviews, telling his secretary in one case: "I would be glad to see him but really do not have the time, and little of what is said to me at audiences stays in my head – but do not tell anyone that." And his answer to interviewees tended always to be the same: "These matters will receive the attention they deserve." He was often still at his desk at midnight, as the despatches from all over the empire piled up on his desk:

I have just been given this other packet of papers from you. I have neither the time nor the strength to look at it, and so will not open it until tomorrow. It is already past ten o'clock and I have not yet dined. My table is full of papers for tomorrow because I cannot cope with any more now.

9 Philip II

A major problem was that Philip trusted paper more than he trusted people. His father had warned him, "transact business with many, and do not bind yourself to or become dependent upon any individual, because although it may save time, it does no good." Philip followed this advice literally, with the consequence that, according to the Secretary to the Council of State,

His Majesty makes mistakes and will continue to make mistakes in many matters because he discusses them with different people, sometimes with one, sometimes with another, concealing something from one minister and revealing it to another. It is therefore small wonder that different and even contradictory decisions are issued.

The failure to delegate also meant that administration of essential matters fell further and further behind, as one of his governors in Italy acidly remarked: "If death came from Spain, we should all live to a very great age."

The strain of work started to tell on Philip's physique. Difficult decisions triggered headaches, though these often seemed to be a delaying tactic. Sometimes he took to his bed. As one court observer rather contemptuously commented, "Whenever the King receives unpleasant and bad news, he suddenly feels ill and suffers from diarrhoea, just like a sheep or rabbit."

Philip was often regarded as a man of implacable will, but there was another side of him. When he was 41 both his insane son, Don Carlos, and his beloved wife, Elizabeth de Valois, died. Philip felt crushed by the demands of life and self-doubt:

They cannot fail to cause pain and exhaustion and, believe me, I am so exhausted and pained by them, and by what happens in this world, that if it were not for things which cannot be abandoned, I do not know what I would do. . . . I know very well that I should be in some other station of life, one not as exalted as the one God has given me, which for me alone is terrible. . . . Please God that in heaven we shall be treated better.

It was in religion that Philip found his only real escape from work. His passion for the authority of the Catholic Church made him seem fanatical. He relished the *auto da fé*, when heretics were burnt, as "something really worth seeing for those who have not seen one". Such sentiments seem inhumane, and yet Philip was driven by an exceptional piety. He spent hours on his arthritic knees, deep in prayer, and he was a kindly, loving man to his family and household. Moreover, it was from religion that Philip drew the strength and conviction to continue his lonely royal duty.

Philip had done nothing about the invasion of England for 15 years after the Pope's call in 1570. Suddenly, he was galvanized by a great sense of urgency, telling his secretary to hurry:

Be quick, so that between tomorrow and Saturday I can be sent the decision which I

10 The Escorial, palace and monastery, built by Philip as a retreat from which to govern the empire. The buildings in the foreground are more recent.

asked for the other day . . . time is passing us by very fast and time lost is never recovered.

As the Pope knew, and Philip could hardly deny, the invasion impulse was more political than religious. Philip himself would have been unable to separate the two: his conviction of special responsibility to God and the Church was total.

These were the characteristics Philip brought to the planning of the Armada. He was meticulous in his work. He knew that the "Invincible Armada" was not, and could not become, invincible. That is why, in 1586, he instructed Parma to assemble an army in the Netherlands for a combined operation in the summer of the following year. He also realized that "although the forces we now have both there [Netherlands] and here [Spanish ports] are insufficient on their own, together – if we can get them together – they will win." Philip was almost certainly right, but he underestimated the difficulty of bringing the two forces together. Nothing was more vital for the Armada plan than for the closest collaboration between the naval and army

11 A Spanish victory in the Netherlands, 1580. Philip was much more concerned about the Netherlands than about England. Note the new defensive style of earthworks, a response to improved artillery.

commanders, but Philip never quite recognized this, handling matters directly with each commander separately. If he himself had been more conversant with the practicalities things might have been all right. But he did not go down to Lisbon to learn from experienced seamen the difficulty of picking up an army off a notoriously dangerous shore, nor did he consider going to the Netherlands with, or without, Santa Cruz, to look at the problem from Parma's viewpoint. Philip was too desk-bound for that. Yet he had a perfect grasp of the problems of engaging the English fleet:

Above all, it must be borne in mind that the enemy's object will be to fight at long distance, in consequence of his advantage in artillery. . . . The aim of our men on the contrary must be to bring him to close quarters and grapple with him.

14

When Philip learnt the fate of the Armada in September 1588 his public stance was stoical – "I sent my fleet against men, not against wind and water" – and he commanded masses to be said to give thanks for those ships that had been saved. Privately, Philip was shattered by God's apparent caprice. However, he quietly went on with his paperwork for the remaining decade of his life. Indeed, despite being confined to a wheelchair, wracked with the pains and incontinence of old age, Philip was still signing papers and initiating new ventures almost to the day he died. To the very last, he could not hand over the reins of power, as one observer commented: "so far from resigning while alive, his Majesty does all he can to rule after he is dead."

Alexander Farnese, Duke of Parma (1545-92)

12 Parma was every bit as intelligent as his portrait suggests.

Alexander Farnese, the Duke of Parma, was probably the greatest soldier of the sixteenth century, with a genius for flexible and unorthodox strategy and tactics. His mother, Margaret, was an illegitimate daughter of Charles V. Parma was, consequently, Philip II's step-nephew, but they disliked and distrusted each other.

Parma had made his military reputation with Don John of Austria in the Netherlands, fighting the Dutch rebels. In September 1578 Don John, on his deathbed, named Parma his successor as commander in the Netherlands. Under his leadership, the Spanish army in the Netherlands began to push back the Dutch rebels in a consistent way. Parma perfected the carrot-and-stick technique, offering generous surrender terms, but also using his army's fearsome reputation, as Sir Roger Williams, a veteran commander with the English army in the Netherlands, bore out: "To speak troth, no Armie that ever I saw, passes that of the Duke de Parma for discipline and good order."

Parma made clever use of bribery. He knew that many of those opposing him, particularly those in the English army, could be bought, and his spies told him exactly who was susceptible. His bribes induced English commanders to surrender major towns: Lier

Tornacum captum anno 1581.

A. Tornacum urbs. B. Propugnaculum martinianu inuaditur et expugnatur.
C. Prin Parmensis aggressionem in muros ordinans. D. Murorum expugnatio.
E. Tornacensium turma Vualloni aggressa reicitur.
F. Ruina veteris casæ ab hostili globo dirutæ Pr Parmensis aliisq conteguntur.
G. Auxiliares copiæ obsessam urbem liberaturæ repelluntur.
H. Pr Parmensis muros circumiens saxis ab urbe iactis sauciatur.
I. Tabellarius quid ei in via acciderit, militibus enarrat.
K. Tornacenses oblatis clauibus urbem Parmenio dedunt.

13 Defenders of a Dutch stronghold offer Parma (on horseback) the keys of the city. Behind are Spanish infantry units, easily the most feared troops in Europe, and in the distance the city is under assault.

(1583), Aalst (1584), Deventer (1587) and St Gertruidenburg (1589). Local noblemen were also bought over. Between 1579 and 1585 he took over 30 major rebel-held towns, with hardly any effort on the part of the Dutch to rescue them. As one rebel commander bitterly wrote when Grave surrendered in 1586, "Everyone knows that the King's golden bullets made a greater breach in the heart of the traitor who commanded it than did the normal battery or any Catholic virtue."

When he was ordered to draw up an invasion plan for England Parma was reluctant. He warned Philip that there were considerable dangers and uncertainties involved; in particular, while his army was in England the French would have little difficulty in seizing the undefended Catholic parts of southern Netherlands.

By early 1587, however, two factors seem to have changed Parma's mind. The execution of Mary Queen of Scots in February may well have put in his mind the possibility of gaining the throne of England himself (on the grounds that he would be in physical control there and that he had a valid claim as Charles V's grandson). Secondly, recent successes suggested that many English could be persuaded to come over to the Catholic side. In January English commanders had betrayed two important strongholds. Parma reported to Philip:

The Zutphen fort . . . and Deventer, which was the real objective of last summer's campaign . . . are thus Your Majesty's at a trifling cost. But what is better, the effect of this treason must be to sow great suspicion between the English and the rebels, so that hereafter no one will know whome to trust.

In spring 1587, therefore, Parma sent Philip his proposal: to send a force of 30,000 infantry

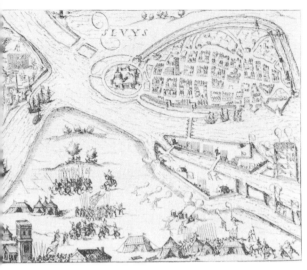

14 Parma captured Sluys in August 1587. "Never," he wrote, "since I came to the Netherlands, has any operation given me such trouble and anxiety as the siege of Sluys." But it was essential for an amphibious operation against England, since it controlled waters deep enough to assemble the flotilla.

15 The English peace commissioners embark to meet Parma in the Netherlands, spring 1588. Parma wanted to reach an agreement with them.

and 4000 cavalry by barge across the Straits of Dover on a calm night. It was an uncharacteristically rash plan, since Parma would risk losing his whole army in mid-Channel. Philip read the plan and filed it with his own verdict scrawled across it: "Hardly possible." He told Parma that he would have to wait for the protection and support of a large and heavily armed fleet from Spain to secure the crossing.

Parma threw himself into the invasion plans with energy. He assembled an army of 30,000 men and undertook the capture of Sluys, an essential port for an amphibious operation against England: "Never since I came to the Netherlands has any operation given me such trouble and anxiety as the siege of Sluys." In summer 1587 Parma was ready and willing, but the Armada failed to appear. Parma wrote to Philip:

Had the Marquis [of Santa Cruz] come when I was first told to look for him, the landing could have been effected without difficulty. Neither the English nor the Dutch were then in a condition to resist your fleet.

Cum his qui oderunt pacem, eram pacificus

English Embaſſ: ſent vnto the Duke of Parma for peace.

During the winter Parma lost heart for the plan, partly because his own force was reduced to 17,000 men through desertion and disease, but also because he had come to see peace with England as the best solution. Philip had ordered him to make a pretence at peace negotiations, but Parma recognized that if the English withdrew from the Netherlands he could probably defeat the Dutch. So, in spring 1588, he warned Philip,

The conquest of England would have been difficult if the country had been taken by surprise. Now they are strong and armed; we are comparatively weak. The danger and the doubt are great; and the English deputies, I think, are really desirous of peace. . . . Since God has been pleased to defer for so long the sailing of the Armada from Lisbon, we are bound to conclude that it is for His greater glory. . . . The enemy have thereby been forewarned and acquainted with our plans, and have made all preparations for their defence.

He also started to distance himself from things if they went wrong:

I am also sure that Your Majesty will have adopted all necessary measures for the carrying out of the task of protecting my passage across [the Straits], so that not the smallest hitch shall occur. . . . Failing this, and the due co-operation of the Duke [of Medina Sidonia] with me, both before and during the actual landing as well as afterwards, I can hardly succeed as I desire in Your Majesty's service.

As if to rub the point in, Parma wrote again in late June about the difficulties of joining up with Medina Sidonia:

With regard to my going out to join him he will plainly see that with these little, low, flat boats, built for these rivers and not for the sea, I cannot diverge from the short direct passage across which has been agreed upon. It will be a great mercy of God indeed if, even when our passage is protected and the Channel free from the enemy's vessels, we are able to reach land in these boats.

Parma was hinting that he would find a reason to prevent his barges putting to sea. In fact, his barges were not in a fit state, but even if they had been he knew they were no match for the Dutch shallow-draft fighting ships waiting to pounce on his force if it put to sea. Furthermore, he failed to reply to the increasingly frantic messages sent by Medina Sidonia as the Armada sailed up the Channel. He did not even leave his inland headquarters at Bruges until after the Armada had met with disaster off Calais.

After the defeat of the Armada Parma made sure it was difficult to pin any specific blame on him. He insisted he had waited for Armada ships to come into the shallows to protect his embarkation. However, Philip must have realized he had been using an unwilling servant.

Parma's career ended in disgrace. In 1591 he was ordered by Philip to invade France. So as not to leave the Dutch rebels free to attack his rear he wrote to Philip for his consent to reach a peace or an armistice, involving religious toleration, with the rebels. This was refused. Meanwhile, he spent part of the money earmarked for the invasion to pay arrears to his mutinous army. Parma's disobedience was not forgiven by Philip, but he was already a sick man, and he died before he could travel to Madrid to face the full consequences of his insubordination.

THE DEFENDERS

The defenders had two vital advantages over their adversaries. They worked under a queen who relied heavily on her advisors, and they either lived in London or visited it frequently. Most of the leading sea captains, like Drake, were in frequent contact with them. Hawkins himself was always on hand, if not in London then at the dockyard at Chatham.

All this did not mean that they worked harmoniously together, imbued with a common purpose. As already mentioned, England's policy-makers were sharply divided between two points of view on how to handle the Spanish threat. Nevertheless, however much they disagreed, the Queen's senior ministers respected each other and were able to disagree amicably, and once war was clearly inevitable they could act as a team.

Sir Francis Walsingham (1532[?]-90)

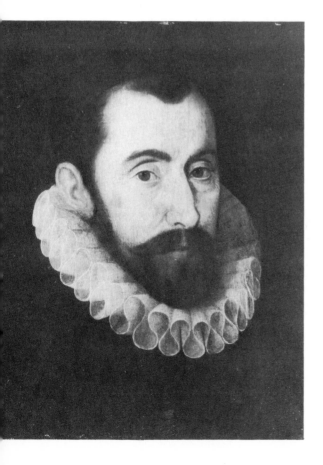

16 Walsingham – shrewd but ruthless.

Walsingham was fiercely Protestant and considered the Catholic powers England's natural enemies. He was, in the Spanish view, "the worst of the heretics". He must have relished this verdict, for the strong religious views instilled in him by his mother were confirmed by travels as a young man in Protestant Germany and Switzerland, and in Catholic Italy, making him, in the words of an observer, "a most sharp maintainer of the purer religion". He came to the notice of William Cecil because of his knowledge of foreign parts and his gift for languages. From his contacts on the Continent he could supply Cecil with the names of those entering England who were hostile to the Crown. In 1569 he gave the earliest warning of the first serious plot, masterminded by Roberto di Ridolfi.

The St Bartholemew's day massacre (1572) of 10,000 or so Parisian Huguenots confirmed Walsingham's view of Catholicism, and his belief that Elizabeth's foreign policy should follow sectarian lines:

What juster cause can a Prince that maketh a profession of the Gospel have to enter into wars that when he seeth confederacies made for the rooting out of the Gospel and the religion he professeth?

Walsingham made his own order of loyalty perfectly clear; "I wish first God's glory, and next the Queen's safety." Such a sentiment could be construed as insufficiently loyal in a servant of the Crown, but he knew how to subordinate his own personal convictions to the dictates of state policy: "I would have all reformation done by public authority. It were very dangerous that every man's zeal should carry sufficient authority of reforming things amiss."

Walsingham tirelessly pursued the Catholic enemy, both in its English and Spanish guise. At home he hunted down Catholic priests, among them the saintly Edmund Campion, but his chief objective was the destruction of Mary Stuart. While she lived, "neither Her Majesty must make account to continue in quiet possession of her crown, nor her faithful servants assure themselves of safety of their lives." English Catholicism threatened the authority of the state, and Walsingham was willing to use torture and execution to extirpate dissidence in the realm. By the end of Elizabeth's reign 181 English Catholics had been executed. National unity was vital.

Our unity might be a strength to ourselves and an aid to our neighbours, but if we shall like to fall to division among ourselves, we must needs lie open to the common enemy and by our own fault hasten, or rather call upon ourselves our own ruin.

When the Ridolfi plot was finally exposed in 1572 it was revealed that part of the plan was for Spain to land an army from the Netherlands to overthrow Elizabeth and install Mary Stuart. Walsingham was convinced that to fight Spain was to do God's will: "The proud Spaniard whom God hath long used for the rod of His wrath I see great hope that He will now cast him into the fire." He supported English privateering attacks on Spanish shipping and urged the Queen to forge an alliance with the Dutch rebels in the Netherlands. His basic argument was that if Spain defeated the Dutch she was bound to turn her attention next to the invasion of England. While living in Paris (1570-3) he had done his best to fuel the Dutch revolt and had thus

. . . given him [the King of Spain] such a bone to pick as would take him up twenty years at least, so that Her Majesty had no more to do but throw into the fire he had kindled some English fuel from time to time to keep it burning.

But it was a good deal harder to persuade the Queen of the wisdom of this hawkish policy, and by 1584 Walsingham was still chafing at the Queen's reluctance to support the rebels fully: "Sorry I am to see the course that is taken in this weighty cause, for we will neither help these poor countries nor yet suffer others to do it."

Only after ten years of urging, did Elizabeth finally agree to send an army to the Netherlands. By then, war with Spain seemed inevitable, but, even so, Walsingham knew she fretted over the cost of war – cost in both human life and money from the royal purse:

These two things being so contrary to Her Majesty's disposition, the one that it breedeth

17 Anthony Babington with his accomplices. Walsingham's interception of Babington's correspondence with Mary Stuart led to her death and his (depicted on the right).

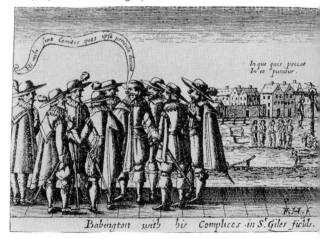

Babington with his Complices in St Giles fields.

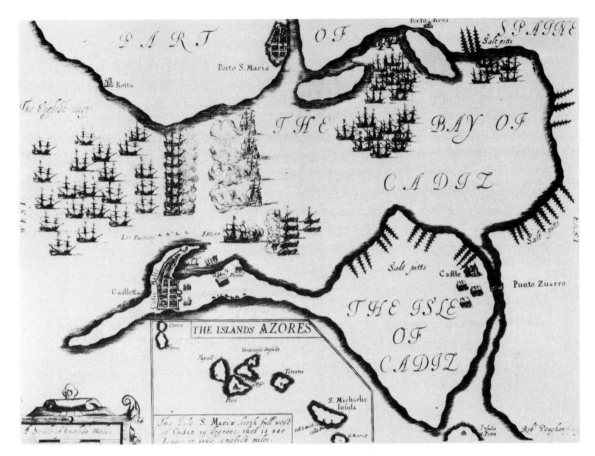

18 "Singeing the King of Spain's beard". Drake's ships entering Cadiz harbour from the left. Seven Spanish galleys are engaged by one English warship near the Isle of Cadiz.

doubt of a perpetual war, the other that it ever requireth an increase of charges, do marvellously distract her and make her repent that ever she entered into the action.

By then, Walsingham was hot on the trail of the last of the Catholic conspiracies. In 1584 he had uncovered Throckmorton's plot but had failed to prove Mary Stuart's complicity. Two years later his agents intercepted correspondence between Mary and a group led by Anthony Babington which clearly showed that she contemplated the overthrow of her cousin. Elizabeth's advisors now insisted on the execution of Mary, but Elizabeth hesitated, unwilling to have the death sentence carried out. Walsingham was beside himself: "I would to God, Her Majesty

would be content to refer these things to them that can best judge of them, as other princes do." Finally she gave way, and Mary was executed in February 1587. By this time, Walsingham was more concerned about Spain's invasion plans and about the preparations in her shipyards. Throughout 1587 his agents kept him well informed of the number and size of ships, the men enlisted, and even full inventories of horses, armour and supplies.

In the first flush of apprehension, Elizabeth agreed to allow Drake, as Walsingham explained to his ambassador in Paris,

. . . to impeach [impede] the joining together of the King of Spain's fleets out of their several ports, to keep victuals from them, to follow them in case they should be come forward towards England or Ireland, and to cut off as many of them as he could and impeach their landing.

Drake's raid on Cadiz could delay the Armada but could not prevent it. As usual,

Walsingham found the Queen deaf to his warnings. She was more interested in snatching peace from the jaws of war and was unwilling to spend money to put the realm on a war footing. She withdrew most of her forces from the Netherlands and refused to blockade the Spanish coast as Walsingham and his seafaring friends recommended. Walsingham despairingly wrote:

The manner of our cold and careless proceeding here in this time of peril maketh me to take no comfort. . . for that I see, unless it shall please God in mercy miraculously to preserve us, we cannot long stand.

He remained critical of Elizabeth's equivocations and expostulated over her refusal to supply the fleet adequately with powder and shot: "Our half doings doth breed dishonour and leaveth the disease uncured."

Walsingham had never enjoyed good health and he died two years later, in 1590. Although Elizabeth found him too abrasive and hawkish in his approach his patriotism was beyond doubt.

William Cecil, Lord Burghley (1520-98)

William Cecil was the leader of the peace party in England. "A realm gains more in one year's peace than by ten years of war" was the maxim of a shrewd and cautious man, and it was these qualities which had made him the Queen's principal minister throughout her long reign. Cecil and Elizabeth wanted to avoid openly committing England to any particular party, be it Protestant or Catholic, pro-French or pro-Spanish. They wanted to secure the English Reformation in a way which would cause offence neither to English Catholics nor to foreign powers. It was a high-wire act.

The dangers were best expressed in the Papal Bull of 1570, which freed Catholics from recognizing Elizabeth as Queen. France and Spain might attack England; Spain had started to feel the provocative effect of England's help to her Dutch rebels; France had cause to support Mary Stuart. At home there was widespread Catholic sentiment. With Mary Stuart as both heir and prisoner of Elizabeth, Catholics were tempted to treason. Lord Burghley, as Cecil had now become, recognized the peril: "I am thrown into a maze at this time, that I know not how to walk from dangers." He also had to contend with the

19 Burghley, dressed as a Knight of the Garter, looking the wise counsellor that he was.

Queen's other advisors, Leicester, Walsingham and Hatton, all of whom advocated a more aggressive policy towards the Catholic powers. He disliked their carefree attitude to illegality. When they urged open support of the Dutch rebels by sending an army to the Netherlands he reminded Elizabeth that it was no more lawful than Spain's encouragement to English Catholics to overthrow their Queen. He similarly deplored the encouragement and financial help given to Drake and his friends for expeditions which were, essentially, piratical.

England's lifeblood was trade with the Continent, and while this flowed mainly through the Spanish Netherlands he counselled, "The Queen of England has more cause to procure the preservation of the Low Countries in their ancient estate." And he warned that if Spain was obliged to regain the Netherlands by conquest Philip would have to levy taxes to pay for it: "And there will be no reason to stop him but he will set what tax he listeth [wishes] upon the commodities of England and so shall England wax [grow] poor to make him rich." However, Burghley also recognized that:

The greatest danger is that when the King of Spain shall have [conquered the Low Countries] he shall be tempted, with the riches thereof to make himself potent with a navy for wars . . . in truth he shall with number of great ships and plenty of mariners, easily overpass all the forces of England.

Burghley's attitude seemed contradictory to those who wanted to support the Dutch rebels. Even after the assassination of William of Orange, when the Dutch looked like collapsing, he and a few others still opposed direct intervention, even though this "incurred heavy displeasure amongst martial men as inclining to the Spaniards' party, degenerate and fainthearted cowards." But Burghley was anything but fainthearted. He recognized perfectly well that sending an army to help the Dutch rebels would be extremely costly and probably achieve little, except to draw Spanish hostility into open war directly against England, and so

. . . held it the best course if the Queen would meddle no more in the matters of the Netherlands, but more strongly fortify her own kingdom, bring the good unto her daily by her innate bounty, restrain the bad, gather money, furnish her navy with all provisions, strengthen the borders towards Scotland . . . and maintain the ancient military discipline of England. So would England become impregnable and she on every side most secure and dreadful to her neighbours.

Seeking to avoid war to the very end, Burghley had actually done more to prepare for war than many of his colleagues. It was he who had started to reorganize the Admiralty Office in the 1560s, and he who had given strong support to peaceful English maritime enterprise, both in trade and exploration. In 1577 he picked out Hawkins to put the navy onto a war footing. On land, too, Burghley ordered "the mustering of all such numbers as have been heretofore chosen and appointed for soldiers", a force estimated at 50,000 infantry and 10,000 horse. After the Armada's defeat Burghley praised these forces for their "generosity and loyalty", but this was only polite propaganda. Burghley had no illusions that the musters were occasions of extravagance and corruption, with captains seeking pay for non-existent soldiers.

By 1586 Burghley, too, viewed war as inevitable but he feared most the dangers within the realm. Like Walsingham, he had urged and obtained Mary Stuart's execution in February 1587, but was exiled from court until June for his pains. He still feared Catholic feeling and in October directed Walsingham to make a list of Catholic recusants in every shire, "that there be such order taken with them as they may do no harm nor be any comfort to the enemy". In January 1588 all these recusants were taken into custody, so that in the event of a Spanish landing they would not be tempted to join with the invaders. He also turned his attention northwards. Because of his weak position, James VI was likely to bend to the stiffest

20 Pen and ink sketch of Mary Stuart's trial. She is depicted twice, entering and seated (A). The empty throne reminds everyone that the court is held by Elizabeth's command.

21 The execution scene. Mary is seen entering (left), preparing herself on the scaffold, and is then executed (scaffold rear).

breeze (see page 68). So he secured James's loyalty during the perilous months with the promise of an English duchy and a pension of £5000 yearly, an offer he quickly withdrew once the danger of invasion subsided.

It is easy to forget the personal constraints, like bereavement and physical decay, on statesmen. Burghley's mother, daughter and wife all died between 1587 and 1589, causing him great grief. By July 1588 Burghley was already an old man, plagued by painful joints: "I hope to get out of my bed this day but not without great pain. As soon as I may be well carried I will endeavour to be brought to court." But get to court he did, and a few days later, as the Armada sailed towards England, he addressed Star Chamber, concluding "with a great exhortation that every man should provide to serve his Queen and his country,

men of peace with looking to peace, men of arms with addressing themselves to arms". It was a characteristic sentiment. When he died, ten years later, his friend William Camden wrote:

Certainly he was a most excellent man who, to say nothing of his reverend presence and undistempered [good tempered] countenance, was fashioned by nature and advanced with learning, a singular man for honesty, gravity, temperance, industry and justice. Hereunto was added a fluent and elegant speech, and that not affected but plain and easy, wisdom strengthened by experience and seasoned with exceeding moderation and most approved fidelity. . . . To speak in a word, the Queen was most happy in so great a Councillor and to his wholesome counsels the state of England for ever shall be beholden.

Sir John Hawkins (1532-95)

The defence of the realm depended upon the creation of a regular navy capable of defeating the Queen's enemies at sea. John Hawkins was pre-eminently well qualified for this task. He came from a Plymouth shipping family and from his youth was intimate with seafaring and shipbuilding. In 1562 he raised capital from friends of his influential father-in-law (the Treasurer to the Navy) to make the first of his "triangular" trading voyages, with the intention of breaking into the Spanish trading monopoly. In West Africa he obtained

> . . . three hundred negroes at the least, besides other merchandises which that country yieldeth . . . with that prey sailed over the Ocean sea unto the Island of Hispaniola [Haiti/Dominica] [where] he received, by way of exchange, hides, gingers, sugars, and some pearls.

He was able to sell these at considerable profit in Europe. On the strength of this venture he made voyages in 1564 and 1567 with the Queen's commission.

His activities soon incurred the displeasure of Spain, and he tried to avoid an open clash, as he knew this would go against Elizabeth's wishes:

> Your Majesty's commandment . . . I have accomplished . . . for I have always been a help to all Spaniards and Portugals that have come in my way without harm or prejudice by me offered to any of them, although many times in this tract they have been under my power.

But Spanish attitudes began to harden. After dining with Hawkins in London, Spain's ambassador reported to Philip:

> This needs decisive action. I could complain to the Queen, but would first like any information you may have from the places [Hawkins] visited. . . . It may be best to dissemble so as to capture and castigate him on the next voyage.

22 Sir John Hawkins.

This is precisely what the Spanish attempted to do. Hawkins and Drake were ambushed at San Juan de Ulloa in 1568. Thanks to their vigilence they escaped to England, but four ships were lost and their crews were killed or captured. Both Drake and Hawkins became implacable enemies of Spain as a result of this incident.

In 1577 Hawkins was appointed Treasurer of the Navy, a post he held for the rest of his life. His report, *Abuses in the Admiralty Touching Her Majesty's Navy, Exhibited by Mr Hawkins*, revealed corrupt and fraudulent practice in the maintenance of the Queen's ships. This led to a vendetta against him by those who were exposed, and he spent some years fighting off accusations of corruption.

Hawkins' reform of the navy was based

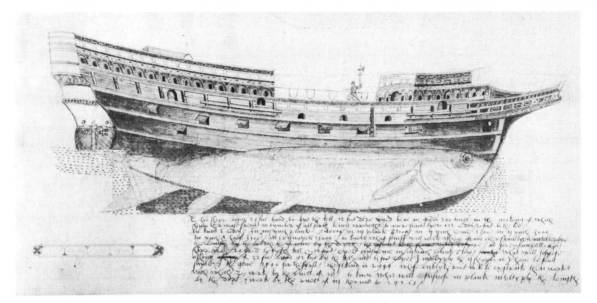

23 Design of a new "race-built" English warship, by one of Hawkins' shipwrights. The fish demonstrates a longer keel, in proportion to the ship's width, making the ship far more nimble.

upon revolutionary strategy and tactics, and on the need for sound financial and administrative procedures. The Navy Board had always conceived the naval defence of the realm to be "to ply up and down" in the Channel and the North Sea, with all ships remaining almost within sight of England and close to fresh food and crew replacements. Hawkins insisted that it was to fight the enemy in her own havens and seas. With regard to Spain he proposed that the best course would be to keep a blockading force of ships off the Spanish coast, to be relieved at four-monthly intervals. The Navy Board did not really accept this theory (which later became the navy's key strategy) but it did allow him to victual ships on the basis of long periods at sea. It also allowed him to redesign the Queen's ships based on his own privateering experience, which persuaded him that the high-built warships still in service, designed for grappling and boarding, were no match for more nimble ships relying solely on gunfire.

His new design, "race-built", removed the castle structures from the bow and stern, making ships less top-heavy and less susceptible to cross and headwinds. He narrowed the width of new-built ships in relation to length from 1:2.5 to 1:3 or 1:4. He also improved the cut of the sails, to make them more manageable and efficient. He revised the manning of ships, affirming the principle that sailors rather than soldiers should be in charge of them and that the crew numbers should be reduced by 25 per cent. With the money he saved he offered higher wages to recruit better quality men.

By this means, Her Majesty's ships would be furnished with able men, such as can shift for themselves, keep themselves clean without vermin and noisomeness, which breedeth sickness and mortality, all which could be avoided. The ships would be able to continue longer in the service that they should be appointed unto, and would be able to carry victuals for a longer time.

Hawkins made a "bargain" with Burghley to maintain the fleet for a lump sum of £4000 yearly, instead of the £6000 previously spent on a piecemeal basis. This cut out those benefiting from corrupt practice, who waged a smear campaign against Hawkins:

The adversaries of the work have continually opposed themselves against me and the service so far as they durst be seen in it, so that among trifling crossings and slanders, the very walls of the realm hath gone . . . to the encouragement of the enemies of God and our country, only to be avenged on me and this

service, which doth discover the corruption and ignorance of time past.

24 Under Hawkins' direction two master shipwrights design new warships.

Burghley had complete confidence and concluded another bargain the following year to increase the number and quality of fighting ships. But Hawkins still faced envious rivals, one of whom wrote to Burghley:

I am sorry to speak it, there is nothing in it but cunning and craft to maintain his pride and ambition, and for the better filling his purse. . . . I perceive your Lordship withstands this Hawkins as much as possible, but he has charmed the Queen, your equals and inferiors.

Hawkins' answer was to bring the navy to a high state of readiness. The whole fleet could put to sea at 21 days' notice, and a smaller force much sooner. At last, Hawkins' main critic, Sir William Wynter, wrote to Burghley,

. . . certifying your Lordship hereby, that he [Hawkins] hath carefully performed the conditions of that offer in such sort that we have no cause to complain of him, but are thoroughly persuaded in our conscience that he hath, for the time since he took over the bargain, expended a far greater sum in carpentry upon Her Majesty's Ships than he hath had any allowance for.

Throughout the last months, while England girded itself against invasion, the government received tributes to Hawkins' work. In February 1588 the Lord Admiral wrote to Burghley:

I have been aboard of every ship that goeth out with me, and in every place where any may creep, and I do thank God that they be in the estate they be in, and there is never a one of them that knows what a leak means . . . [they] shall prove arrant liars that have reported the contrary.

If Hawkins was satisfied with his efforts to prepare the navy for war he was a good deal less satisfied with attention given to his

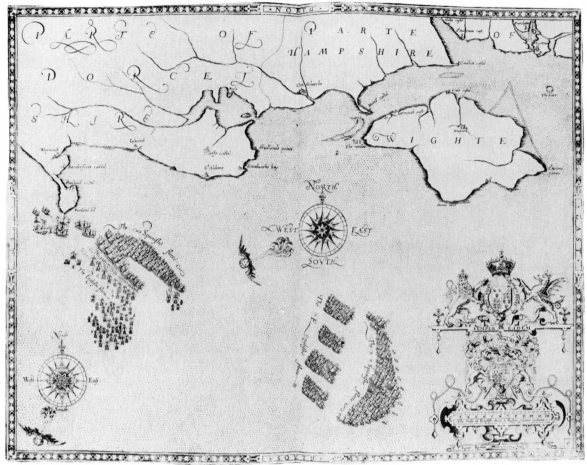

25 Hawkins' participation in the Armada battles. This map show the battle off Portland Bill, and the chase the following day, when the English fleet was divided into four divisions for the first time. Hawkins commanded one of these. Note the coat of arms of Elizabeth and that of Lord Howard below it.

strategic and tactical advice. His own experience, and the later exploits of Drake, particularly his 1585 raid through the Caribbean, confirmed the validity of his offensive strategy:

We have to choose either a dishonourable and uncertain peace, or put on virtuous and valiant minds, to make a way through with such a war as may bring forth and command a quiet peace.

And this to Hawkins meant a blockade of Spain and control of the Atlantic. It is likely his support helped obtain approval for Drake's raid on Cadiz in 1587.

In 1588 Hawkins joined the English fleet at sea as third in rank, under the Lord Admiral and his deputy, Drake. He distinguished himself during the battles in the Channel and was knighted for his service. After the Armada Hawkins tried to retire, but he was not allowed to. He died at sea during a disastrous expedition to the West Indies in 1595. Like Drake, he was spared returning to face Elizabeth's displeasure.

THE COMBATANTS

For centuries the Armada commander has been dismissed as an incompetent coward and the English commander has been eclipsed by his vice admiral, Sir Francis Drake. It is a grossly distorted picture. Both commanders were humble enough to recognize the superior seafaring experience of their subordinates, but in no sense did they shirk the burden of command, and, as importantly, they also ably ensured harmony among their sea captains, where friction might well have arisen.

No commanders have ever had to cope with the problems they faced, of which keeping the fleet victualled and healthy figured far more prominently in their minds than the relatively brief moments of conflict.

It was the first major clash of fleets of sailing ships, and both commanders found themselves grappling with the challenge of effective seamanship and gunnery on the grand scale. Medina Sidonia discovered first the major problem his high-built ships had in sailing against the wind. The Armada had set sail from Lisbon on 30 May, but was almost immediately struck by strong west-north-westerly wind which, according to the pilots, blew the Armada almost as far as Cape St Vincent – in the *opposite* direction. Three weeks later the Armada put in to Corunna to refit, to revictual – much of the food having been found to be rotten – and to replace those who had already fallen sick. These things were not new phenomena, but never before had they happened on such a scale. It is unlikely the English fleet would have fared so badly.

26 Map showing the Armada's progress up the Channel.

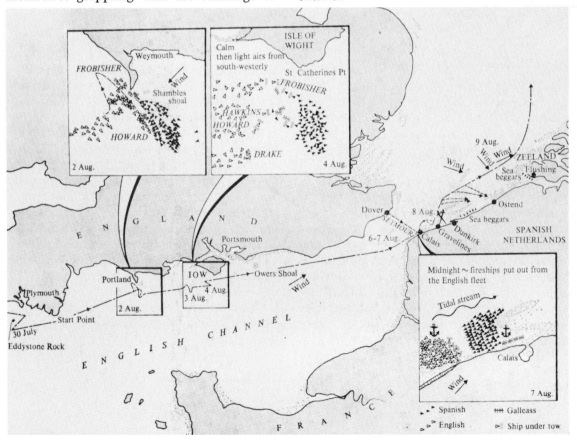

27 A contemporary view of the battle of Gravelines.

Hawkins' redesign of ships and sails made it far more able to withstand bad weather and able to sail significantly closer to an adverse wind than the Armada.

Two other discoveries were made. The first concerned the need to sail large groups of ships in tight formation. The Armada's orderliness contrasts with the ragged chase at first given by the English fleet, and it was only half way up the Channel that the English realized that similar discipline was a vital requirement. The final discovery made, but not really learnt, was that England's superiority in artillery was partly illusory. All the way up the Channel the English fired their longer-range culverins just outside the range of the Spanish medium-range cannon. This was the intelligent thing to do, but the resulting damage to Spanish ships was negligible. At the decisive battle of Gravelines, on 8 August, the English decided to fight at far closer range, and they immediately started to inflict serious damage. It was also at Gravelines that Drake initiated a tactic that subsequently became a classic of attack. He led his ships in line past an enemy ship, each firing its broadside, and then the line turned about to deliver another series of shots. But it was not until considerably later that this became a standard tactic in the navy. In fact, the English would have done far better with the Spanish cannon, which though only medium-range had heavier shot, than with culverins. But neither side fully realized that heavier shot was essential to smash ships, a fact not fully appreciated until well into the next century.

Don Alonzo Perez de Guzman el Bueno, Duke of Medina Sidonia (1550-1611)

Command of the forthcoming Armada was the last thing the Duke of Medina Sidonia ever wanted or expected. On his estate near Cadiz he lived a quiet life with no interest in warfare. But he was hereditary Captain General of Andalusia, and in this capacity had proved himself barely a year earlier by rapidly marshalling land forces to prevent Drake landing at Cadiz. He was also Spain's senior duke and, when Santa Cruz died, this destined him to his unhappy command. When he read Philip's letter of appointment he penned a reply that from any other hand might have seemed disrespectful:

Sir, I have no health for the sea, for I know from the small experience which I have had that I am easily seasick and catch cold. . . . Apart from this neither my conscience nor my duty will allow me to undertake this service. The fleet is so large, and the undertaking so important, that it would be wrong for a person like myself, with no experience of seafaring or warfare, to take charge of it.

But Philip would not listen to excuses:

The undertaking being so important . . . and my own affairs depending so greatly upon its success, I had not wanted to place so weighty a matter in any hands but yours. Such is my confidence in you personally, and in your experience and desire to serve me that I look for the success we aim at.

In many ways, Philip's judgement was correct. Medina Sidonia had a quietness of mind and humility to make best use of his sea captains and to maintain harmony among them. He created a tight Armada formation, which was later to dismay the English, but keeping the fleet together meant "governing

28 Medina Sidonia, in his sixties, almost 30 years after the Armada's defeat.

our progress by the speed of the most miserable tub among us". Slow and vulnerable, the cargo ships turned the Armada from a fighting force into a convoy, making Philip's instructions for battle quite impossible:

I have only to press upon you not to miss the gaining of every possible advantage, and so to order the Armada that all parts of it shall be able to fight and lend mutual assistance. . . . Above all, it must be borne in mind that the enemy's object will be to fight at long distance, in consequence of his advantage in artillery. . . . The aim of our men, on the contrary, must be to bring him to close quarters and grapple with him, and you will have to be very careful to have this carried out.

As a result of the storms which scattered many ships outside Lisbon and forced a refit in Corunna, Medina Sidonia made one last attempt to dissuade his sovereign from the enterprise:

. . . seeing matters in their present state, I feel compelled by my diligent duty to Your Majesty to submit the following points for consideration. . . . We have now arrived in this port [Corunna] so scattered and shaken that we are much inferior in strength to the enemy, in the opinion of all who are competent to judge.

29 First sighting of England, off the Lizard on 29 July. The English pinnace which spotted the Armada may also be seen making for Plymouth.

He had the backing of his commanders, who echoed his unease:

In this enterprise His Majesty had embarked all his naval force existing in these seas; and in case of misfortune, either in warfare or tempest, the whole was liable to be lost, as is proved in the present condition of affairs.

So Medina Sidonia concluded his appeal to Philip:

How do you think we can attack so great a country as England with such a force as ours is now? I have earnestly commended this matter to God, and feel bound to lay it before Your Majesty, so that you can choose the best course while the Armada is refitting here. This opportunity can be taken, and the difficulties avoided, by making honourable terms with the enemy.

Philip could not consider a course that might be seen as a weakness of resolve. He therefore

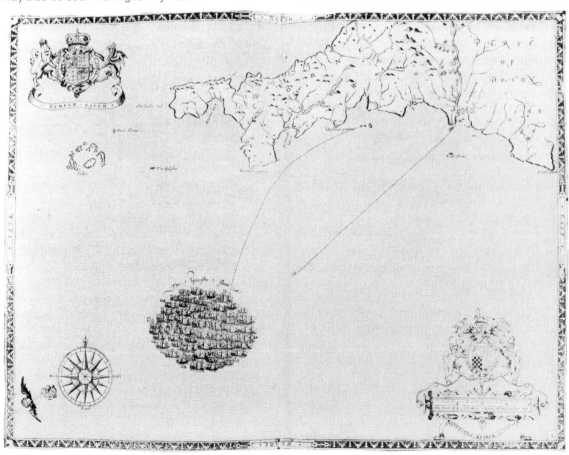

30 The battle off the Isle of Wight. Note the crescent-shaped Armada formation, more disciplined than the English, and the galleass in the foreground.

commanded Medina Sidonia to set sail again as soon as possible.

Medina Sidonia did not question Philip again, but followed his instructions precisely, in particular:

It is important that you and the Duke [of Parma] should be mutually informed of each other's movements, and it will therefore be advisable that before you arrive thither you should continue to communicate with him as best you can.

Medina Sidonia sent his first pinnace (a small, lightly armed ship used for scouting and conveying messages) to warn Parma of his approach on 25 July, three days out from Corunna. Within sight of the Lizard, Medina Sidonia still had no response from Parma, so he wrote to Philip:

Without information from him, I can only proceed slowly. . . . All along the coast of Flanders there is no harbour to shelter our ships, and if I took the

Armada there from the Isle of Wight it might be driven onto the shoals.

The Isle of Wight was his last safe haven before the rendezvous with Parma off the dangerous sandbanks of the Netherlands:

To avoid such an obvious danger, I have decided to stay off the Isle of Wight until I know what the duke is doing, as the plan is that the moment I arrive he should come out with his fleet, without making me wait for a minute.

But he could not stop, for Philip had already told him "On no account will you enter the Wight on your way up, nor before you have made every possible effort to carry out the main idea."

After the inconclusive battles in the Channel, off Eddystone lighthouse on 31 July, off Portland Bill on 2 August and off the Isle of Wight on 4 August, neither side had much ammunition left. The English could replenish from the coast, but Medina Sidonia could only replenish with Parma's help, so he sent a more urgent message:

My stores are beginning to run short with these constant skirmishes, and if . . . the enemy continues his tactics, as he certainly will, it will be advisable . . . to load a couple of ships with powder and ball of the sizes noted in the enclosed memorandum, and to despatch them to me without the least delay.

But his worst fear was that Parma was not ready to embark:

It will also be advisable for Your Excellency to make ready at once to put out to meet us, because by God's grace, if the wind serves, I expect to be on the Flemish coast very soon.

Medina Sidonia had repeatedly been told by Philip to rendezvous with Parma at sea or to meet him "off Cape Margate". As the Armada dropped anchor off Calais, he made a last desperate plea for flyboats (shallow-draft fighting ships) to help protect the Armada till Parma was able to get to sea:

I am anchored here, two leagues from Calais with the enemy's fleet on my flank. They can cannonade me whenever they like, and I shall be unable to do them much harm in return. If you can send me forty or fifty flyboats of your fleet I can, with their help, defend myself here until you are ready to come out.

In fact, Parma was still in Bruges, and, according to Cabrera de Cordoba, one of his emissaries, he "acted as if he did not believe that the news of the Armada's coming could be true". Indeed, before Parma's army had started to embark the Armada had been defeated – by fireships on the night of 7 August and by English gunnery the following day. Only by a miraculous change of wind did the Armada escape the Netherlands' sandbanks. A strong south-westerly wind left Medina Sidonia with only one option:

We have sailed with the same wind . . . it has been impossible for us to return to the English Channel even if we desired to do so. We have now, the 20th August, doubled the last of the Scottish islands to the north, and we have set our course with a NE wind for Spain. (*Calendar of State Papers [Spanish]*)

Medina Sidonia's ship reached Spain on 23 September, after a month of being buffetted by the severe storms on the west coast of the British Isles. He had already sent a pinnace ahead to explain that "Our Lord has seen fit to dispose matters differently from that which had been expected." Medina Sidonia was too ill to get ashore unaided. He had to be carried. He reported: "The trouble and miseries we have suffered cannot be described. . . . They

31 The crucial night of 7/8 August, when the English (left) sent their fireships (centre) to break up the Armada (right) at anchor off Calais (foreground right).

have been worse than have ever been seen in any voyage before.'' Within the month, Medina Sidonia had obtained permission to return home. He was so weak he had to be carried in a horse litter. It took another six months for him to recover physically. It is doubtful he ever recovered mentally or emotionally from his ordeal.

Juan Martinez de Recalde (1526-88)

After Santa Cruz, Juan Martinez de Recalde was unquestionably the finest seaman in Spain, and on Santa Cruz's death Recalde was the obvious candidate to see the Armada plan successfully executed. He can hardly have welcomed his commission. He was already 62 years old and he suffered greatly from sciatica. However, he could not have expected to command the venture. Although a knight of Santiago, he was not of sufficiently noble birth. In a world where nobility dictated precedence, Recalde's authority would not have been acceptable to higher-born subordinates. He accepted this state of affairs, but he deplored the way in which rank rather than ability characterized much of the Armada's military force, and he wrote to Philip II to say so:

I hear great complaints about the command of companies being given to young fellows just because they are gentlemen. Very few of them are soldiers or know what to do, and their officers are no better.

There is no sign that Recalde felt this about his own commander, Medina Sidonia, and he knew that the latter relied heavily on his sound advice, as Vice Admiral, to help him in this unusually difficult expedition.

Recalde was well aware that the mission verged on the impossible. When the Papal legate asked how the Armada could be sure of winning it was he, almost certainly, who answered, tongue in cheek:

It's very simple. It is well known that we fight in God's cause. So when we meet the English, God will surely arrange matters so that we can grapple and board them, either by sending

32 Juan Martinez de Recalde.

some strange freak of weather or, more likely, just by depriving the English of their wits.

No hardened old Biscayan salt like Recalde could possibly believe in such things, and he gave a more hard-headed answer, too:

Unless God helps us with a miracle the English, who have faster and handier ships than ours, and many more long-range guns, and who know their advantage just as well as we do, will never close with us at all, but stand off and knock us to pieces with their culverins, without our being able to do them any serious hurt. So we are sailing against England in the confident hope of a miracle.

Recalde immediately saw the flaws in Philip's plan. When Medina Sidonia held a council of war in Corunna, whilst refitting after their disastrous start, it was Recalde who put forward the sound tactical viewpoint, essentially what his old mentor Menendez de

33 Plymouth was the perfect harbour. Recalde had wanted to seize one of Devon's numerous natural harbours as a firm base from which to invade England. (From a contemporary chart)

Aviles (see page 66) would have advised – the seizure of a firm base on English soil as close as possible to Spain. Recalde's authority on naval tactics was unsurpassed, and it was he who was asked to argue with Philip for a sounder plan. Having rehearsed in his mind Philip's plan and the foreseeable difficulties of implementation, he tactfully put his finger on some of the problems:

From the mouth of the Thames to Southampton – about 40 leagues – I know of no port capable of taking large vessels, all the coast being very uninviting. The harbours of Southampton and the Isle of Wight are well defended by forts.

Landing troops in the West Country seemed far sounder than a hazardous rendezvous with Parma somewhere in the Straits of Dover:

It appears to me that the most convenient and easiest ports for landing would be Falmouth, Plymouth, or Dartmouth, especially as the highly

necessary reinforcements of men and stores will have to be sent from Spain, and isolated vessels will be exposed to much danger higher up the Channel.

As he pointed out,

In the case of our encountering and defeating the enemy, I feel sure that he will not suffer so much damage as to be unable to repair, at all events sufficiently to impede the passage of our reinforcements high up the Channel. But it will be difficult for him to do this if our Armada be stationed in the above-mentioned ports lying nearest to Spain. If it be possible for the reinforcement to be sent in strength sufficient to attack those ports, whilst the conquest is being affected higher up, that will be the best course.

34 The opening battle on 31 July. Recalde, on the landward flank, tries to draw the English attackers into a close melée in which the Spanish would prove stronger. To the right, the two fleets move on after the first encounter.

In other words, Recalde wanted a plan in which the Armada would still assist Parma's army across the Straits but only after the seizure of a West Country port. The invasion of England would be a two-pronged attack, the Armada-borne army (and subsequent reinforcements) advancing out of the West Country, and Parma's army advancing from Margate. Inevitably, Recalde's suggestion went unheeded.

A lesser man might have resented Philip's disregard for his professional advice. But Recalde's conduct throughout the whole campaign was one of loyalty, courage and seamanship. He was in command of the rearguard, protecting the landward and more vulnerable flank. In the first fight with the English fleet off Eddystone Recalde drew the enemy on to himself, and one must speculate that he hoped the English would be enticed to grapple and board him, so giving the other Armada ships time to close in and grapple, for he said: "If we can come to close quarters, Spanish valour and Spanish steel (and the great masses of soldiers we have on board) will make our victory certain."

All the way up the Channel, and throughout the crucial battle of Gravelines on 8 August, Recalde was one of the first to bring help where it was most needed. By the time the Armada was sailing north through the North Sea Recalde was a very sick man, confined to his bunk. It was probably no accident, however, that he was one of the very few to have put in to the Irish shore and sailed away again without being shipwrecked. His ship made landfall close to Smerwick Harbour, where, in 1580, he had landed a small Spanish force from six ships to assist the Irish rebels against the English. Recalde struggled from his sickbed and guided his ship through the perilous rocks into Blasket Sound. Eight of his men, who went ashore to find water and were captured by English soldiers, admitted to them:

There are eighty soldiers and twenty of the mariners sick, and the Captain [Recalde] very sad and weak. . . . There is left in this flagship . . . no water but what they brought out of Spain which stinketh marvellously, and the meat they cannot eat. . . . The admiral's purpose is with the first wind to pass to Spain.

Recalde tried to get another water party ashore but "they found only great rocks with the sea pounding against them, and saw a hundred armed men marching along the cliffs, carrying a white standard with a red cross."

Finally, a little water was obtained from a small stream on the shore, and a few days later the weather allowed Recalde to sail back to Spain. The final struggle to reach home proved too much for this gallant but sick old man. Four days after reaching Corunna and completing his duty he died in his bunk. Neither Philip nor Medina Sidonia could have hoped for a finer servant.

Charles, Lord Howard of Effingham (1536-1624)

Like Medina Sidonia, Howard was appointed Lord Admiral on account of his nobility. He was the Queen's first cousin once removed and had married another of her first cousins.

Howard was more fortunate than his counterpart, for he had some experience of the sea. He first went to sea under the direction of his father, the then Lord Admiral, during Queen Mary's reign. In 1570 he commanded a strong squadron in the Channel to honour the

DESIR. NA. REPOS

HONI· SOIT· QVI· MAL·Y·PENSE

The right Honorable Charles Earle
of Nottingham Baron of Effingham Lo.
high Admirall of England Irelande
and of y principly Islip of Wales Knight of y
most noble order of y garter & latin to y m
of ad her ma. Highly parke and chaces on
this syde Trent constable of y honorable
castle of Windsor Lieutennant generall of
Suffex & Surrey & on of her M prince councell

Anno Domin
1588

Claſſem inuincibilem tibi Carole hic Philip
Tradidit Hiſpani victam Deus, Arma, Malyne
Sēruit inſani, Maris aſtus Numine ſacro
Virtus Genuiſ, tui, Sed Hcnc, hæc amplis
Te ſpoliis, Ducem reducem videmus omnium.

To be ſoulde at y horſeſhoe in paternoster row

Si domitos Bello Hiſpanos, Gadiumq́; ruinam,
Indomitum ſi Marte virum, Patriǽq́; Parentem.

Conſilio fortem ſi quæris: En Hos tibi ſculpta
Magnanimi effigies Caroli depingit Houardi.

Queen of Spain who was travelling to the
Netherlands, and to prevent any treachery on
the part of the Spanish naval escort. In May
1585 he became Lord Admiral, an office
which he relished. He delighted in his ships:

35 Lord Howard of Effingham.

"I protest before God and as my soul shall
answer for it, that I think there were never in
any place of the world worthier ships than

these are." He was particularly pleased with his own flagship, *Ark Royal*, built privately by Walter Raleigh and purchased by Hawkins for the navy:

Tell Her Majesty from me that her money was well given for the Ark Ralegh, for I think her the odd ship in the world for all conditions, and truly I think there can no great ship make me change and go out of her.

Nothing was harder for Howard and his colleagues than waiting for Spain's invasion. Bad weather kept the English fleet in port.

I protest before God I would I had not a foot of land in England, that the wind would serve us to be abroad; and yet it is a hard matter and a thing unpossible for us to lie in any place to guard England.

And if the English fleet should get to sea, what should it do? "The surest way to meet with the Spanish fleet is upon their own coast, or in any harbour of their own, and there to defeat them." Howard felt sure the Spanish had delayed their invasion for a purpose:

I am verily persuaded they mean nothing else but to linger it out upon their own coast, until they understand that we have spent our victuals here, and therefore we must be busy with them before we suffer ourselves to be brought to that extremity.

He had a point. Keeping the whole fleet on indefinite standby was a logistical nightmare. Because of the problem of victualling the fleet, he and Hawkins had willingly agreed to keep it at only half strength during the winter months.

Elizabeth, however, sent Howard sharp word not to go to Spain but to patrol the Channel. Howard was stung by her rebuke, and freely admitted he had once been of the Queen's present opinion, just as she had once favoured attacking the Spanish coast:

You know it hath been the opinion both of Her Majesty and others, that it was the surest course

36   Howard's flagship, the *Ark Royal*.

to lie on the coast of Spain. I confess my error at that time, when my opinion was otherwise; but I did and will yield ever unto them of greater experience.

Howard refused to give way and Elizabeth reluctantly agreed to his proposal. But when he sailed for Spain in July the wind dropped 60 or so miles from the coast and then blew up strongly from the south, persuading the English fleet to return home. As it turned out, this was fortuitous, for "The southerly wind that brought us back from the coast of Spain brought them [the Armada ships] out. God blessed us with turning us back."

On 29 July, barely a week after his return to Plymouth, Howard learnt that the Armada was approaching:

I received intelligence that there were [sic.] a great number of ships descried off the Lizard; whereupon, although the wind was very scant, we first warped out of harbour that night, and upon Saturday turned out very hardly, the wind being South West; and about three of the clock

37 Howard's manoeuvre that dismayed the Spanish so much. This contemporary map shows how the English fleet was able to "gain the wind", having tacked during the night of 30 July. Some of the fleet sailed across the front of the Armada and can be seen rejoining the rest of the English fleet to pursue the Armada. The strength of the Armada formation is also clearly shown.

in the afternoon, descried the Spanish fleet, and did what we could to work for the wind, which by this morning we had recovered, descrying their fleet to consist of 120 sail.

Howard's account of the very tricky operation to get out of Plymouth Sound against a fresh south-westerly is typically modest. In fact, it required not only nimble ships but considerable skill. It is unlikely the Armada could have made headway in similar circumstances.

Once he had gained the wind, during the night of 30 July, a feat that utterly dismayed the Spanish, Howard was able to commence battle:

38 When the Armada was first sighted off the Lizard a series of beacons was lit across the country to warn the people of England. Most of these beacons were probably bonfires, as can be seen across the hillside (left).

At nine of the clock we gave them fight, which continued until one. In this fight we made some of them to bear room to stop their leaks; notwithstanding we durst not adventure to put among them, their fleet being so strong.

Howard was appalled by the strength of the Spanish formation. He realized that he faced a running battle up the Channel, requiring far

more ammunition than he had. He urgently appealed for more: "For the love of God and the country, let us have with some speed some great shot sent us of all bigness; for this service will continue long; and some powder with it." One can forgive Howard his outrage when he was instructed to submit an inventory of his requirements. He must have cursed the bureaucratic state of mind of civil servants:

I have received your letter wherein you desire a proportion of shot and powder to be set down by me and sent unto you; which by reason of the uncertainty of the service [battle], no man can do; therefore I pray you to send with all speed as much as you can.

Howard's only serious misjudgment followed the success of the fireships at Calais. The next day he could not resist chasing a

39 Close engagement during the battle of Gravelines (8 August) between Howard's *Ark Royal* and the *Rata*, commanded by Don Alonso de Leyva, who perished on the Irish coast. Although the ships engaged more closely than before, they were certainly not as close as this picture suggests.

warship as it made for safety in Calais. He should have been leading the attack on the rest of the Armada. However, his fleet served him well, for although few Spanish ships were sunk they were badly battered by English guns and were obliged to escape northwards. Neither Howard nor his colleagues recognized that the Armada was already decisively defeated. He still feared further engagements:

We have chased them in fight until this evening late, and distressed them much; but their fleet consisteth of mighty ships and great strength. . . . Their force is wonderful great and strong, and yet we pluck their feathers by little and little.

As the Armada sailed up the North Sea, Howard and his commanders

. . . determined and agreed in council to follow and pursue the Spanish fleet until we have cleared our own coast and brought the Firth west of us; and then to return back again, as well to revictual our ships, which stand in extreme scarcity, as also to guard and defend our own coast at home.

England had expected a more resounding demonstration of seamanship and gunnery.

Some criticized Howard's handling of the fleet, for fighting by gunfire rather than grappling and boarding was still a novel tactic, but Sir Walter Raleigh defended him as

. . . better advised than a great many malignant fools were that found fault with his demeanour. The Spaniards had an army aboard them and he had none; they had more ships than he had, and of higher building and charging; so that had he entangled himself with those great and powerful vessels, he had greatly endangered this kingdom of England. . . . But our admiral knew his advantage and held it; which had he not done, he had not been worthy to have held his head.

Howard had little opportunity to enjoy the victory. For weeks he was busy with the repair and refitting of ships, paying off ship crews, and the distressing business of dealing with a major epidemic which killed many seamen during August and September that year.

Howard remained Lord Admiral until 1619. Until Elizabeth's own death in 1603, and the subsequent end of the Spanish war, Howard was busy arranging the sea and coastal defence of the realm and equipping the various expeditions against Spanish-held-territories.

Sir Francis Drake (1540-96)

Because of his unrivalled seamanship, Drake had expected to be given effective command of the English fleet, leaving Lord Howard only nominal control. In the event, he was given command of the western fleet based at Plymouth, which guarded the approaches to the British Isles. He was itching to strike Spain as he had done a year earlier, but the Queen was desperately striving to avert conflict by negotiating with the Duke of

Parma. Drake was beside himself and wrote to her Council:

My very good Lords, next under God's mighty protection, the advantage and gain of time and place will be the only and chief means for our good; wherein I most humbly beseech your good Lordships to persevere as you have begun, for that with fifty sail of shipping we shall do more good upon their own coast, than a great

many more will do here at home; and the sooner we are gone, the better we shall be able to impeach [impede] them.

Drake was undoubtedly correct in his assessment, but the Council did not respond, so he wrote again, this time to Elizabeth herself:

If Your Majesty will give present order for our proceeding to the sea, and send to the strengthening of this fleet here four more of Your Majesty's good ships, and those 16 sail of ships with their pinnaces which are preparing in London, then shall Your Majesty stand assured, with God's assistance, that if the fleet come out of Lisbon, as long as we have victual to live withal upon that coast, they shall be fought with ... in such sort as shall hinder his quiet passage into England.

40 Sir Francis Drake.

41 A Victorian view of Drake's game of bowls. In fact, there was no hurry, because the English fleet could not get out of Plymouth for another six hours, after the tide had changed.

And Drake ended his request with the irrefutable warning: "The advantage of time and place in all martial actions is half a victory; which being lost is irrecoverable."

This was Drake at his most articulate. He usually expressed himself on paper far more clumsily. It is unlikely that Elizabeth's Council doubted his tactical grasp, but it doubted its man. Drake was offering to defeat the Armada alone, reducing the Lord Admiral to mere titular authority, and risking envy among his peers: Hawkins, Frobisher and Fenner. Nor did the Council altogether trust Drake to obey orders strictly. He had a tendency to shoot off on his own brilliant meteoric course. So it sent Howard from Margate to Plymouth with the main fleet to join Drake and take over command. Drake, to his credit, submitted with a good grace. Howard appreciated his gracious behaviour, writing to Walsingham:

Sir, I must not omit to let you know how lovingly and kindly Sir Francis Drake beareth himself; and also how dutifully to her Majesty's service and unto me, being in the place I am in, which I pray you he may receive thanks for, by some private letter by you.

Drake proved a loyal subordinate, "always of one mind and thought with the senior admiral, although there were those who had thought, or maybe feared, a different outcome".

Once the Armada had sailed into the Channel and battle had been joined, Howard was sensitive to Drake. He gave him the honour of leading the pursuit of the Armada on the night of 31 July. Drake, in the *Revenge*, was to lead the whole English fleet by the great poop lantern on his stern. Suddenly, in the darkness, the light went out. The truth was that Drake deliberately extinguished his lantern in order to leave the fleet and capture a crippled Spanish galleon, the *Nuestra Seniora del Rosario*. He rejoined the fleet at dawn. Drake's conduct might have been disastrous, as one observer commented:

Our own fleet, being disappointed of their light, by reason that Sir Francis Drake left the watch to pursue certain hulks . . . lingered behind, not knowing whom to follow; only his Lordship [Howard] . . . pursued the enemy all night within culverin shot; his own fleet being as far behind

42 An early eighteenth-century engraving showing Drake's capture of the *Nuestra Seniora del Rosario* ("Our Lady of the Rose") at dawn on 1 August. Drake had left his station, leading the fleet, and Howard and two other ships are dangerously close to the Armada. The rest of the English fleet were much further away than this picture suggests.

as, the next morning, the nearest might scarce be seen half-mast high, and very many out of sight, which with a good sail recovered not his Lordship the next day before it was very late in the morning.

Curiously, Drake was not blamed for this irresponsible act, but it does give substance to the Council's misgivings in allowing Drake freedom to act on his own initiative.

It was characteristic that those unaware of Howard's real authority assumed Drake was in command. In Paris it was reported:

For four days Drake continuously kept to windward of the enemy, thanks to better sailing of his ships, and pursued and bombarded them without ceasing. He can repeat this manoeuvre as often as he pleases, for the Spanish ships are heavy and difficult to handle.

Howard, Drake, Hawkins and Frobisher must have discussed their failure to make their superior gunnery count. They realized that they had to get far closer to the enemy ships if they were going to cause the damage essential to the dispersal and destruction of the Armada

43 Don Pedro de Valdes surrenders the *Rosario* and its crew to Drake, as depicted by a Victorian artist. De Valdes spent the next few months in London as an honoured prisoner. His crew was given a far rougher time, and was used virtually as slave labour on a Devon estate.

as a fighting force. On the morning after the Armada was dispersed by fireships Drake led his division in line to pour a broadside at very close range into the *San Martin*, the Armada flagship. He then turned about to come round again and give a second broadside. He was pleased with the results of this eight-hour long battle, which had left both fleets exhausted of ammunition:

God hath given us so good a day in forcing the enemy so far to leeward as I hope in God the Prince of Parma and the Duke of Sidonia shall not shake hands this few days; and whensoever they shall meet, I believe neither of them will greatly rejoice of this day's service.

The following day, Drake was in hot pursuit of the Armada:

We have them before us and mind with the grace of God to wrestle a pull with him. There was never anything pleased me better than seeing the enemy flying with a southerly wind to the northwards. God grant you may have a good eye to the Duke of Parma, for with the grace of God, if we live, I doubt not but 'ere it will be long so to handle the matter with the Duke of Sidonia as he shall wish himself at St Mary Port [his home near Cadiz] among his orange trees.

Drake was a convinced and ardent Protestant. His vendetta against Spain had always also been a religious crusade, and when he wrote in religious terms they must be taken to be most sincerely meant, especially when addressed to Walsingham, who shared his ardour:

Let us all with one accord praise God, the only giver, who of His only will hath sent this proud enemy of His truth where he hath tasted of His power, as well by storm and tempest.

Drake's reputation never reached the same heights again. In 1589 he and the veteran soldier Sir John Norris attacked Portugal, with the intention of ousting Spanish rule there. But they were relying on a local rising which never materialized. Only 6000 of a total complement of 23,000 returned alive. In 1595 he and Hawkins made another expedition to the West Indies, but it proved a disaster. Hawkins died in November, and Drake in January 1596, both of dysentery. Drake was buried at sea.

Soldiers and Mariners

In many respects the ordinary mariners, Spanish and English, had more in common with each other than with those who commanded them. A mariner's life was, in the words of an old sea captain, Luke Fox: "to endure and suffer, as a hard cabin, cold and salty meat, broken sleeps, mouldy bready, dead beer, wet clothes, want of fire, all these are within board". Few put to sea willingly, as a Portuguese prisoner explained:

I was at mine own house, which is 70 leagues from Lisbon. . . . In the kingdom of Portugal there was no preparation of men; but when they embarked themselves, they commanded 2,000 Portingals [Portuguese] to go aboard on pain of death.

Things were similar in England, as a pressing commission of 1589 shows:

We (Elizabeth, by the Grace of God etc)

therefore . . . do give full Power and Authority unto the said Sir Martin Frobisher . . . wheresoever he shall have need to press and take up for service to the Furniture of such ships as are committed to his charge . . . and punish by Imprisonment such as shall be found disobedient and shall obstinately inpugn such good Orders as are usually observed in our Navies and Armies on the Seas . . .

Often, the only men who could be pressed were incapable of service, being old or unfit. Refitting in Corunna, Medina Sidonia reported:

The captains themselves refuse to have anything to do with them – it is obvious all the use they would be is to die on board the ships and take up space. Not a soul of them knows what an arquebus [a portable gun] is, or any other weapon, and already they are more dead than alive."

44 A Spanish officer and infantryman of the period. The Armada carried 20,000 soldiers.

Discipline at sea was strict. Medina Sidonia ordered his captains

. . . to take particular care that no soldier, sailor, or other person in the Armada shall blaspheme, or deny Our Lord, Our Lady, or the Saints, under very severe punishment to be inflicted at our discretion.

And similar instructions were issued to English ships. Those who blasphemed or swore were punished by a marlin spike (a pointed metal tool) which was "clapt into their mouths and tied behind their heads, and then [they were made] to stand a whole hour, till their mouths be very bloody".

Everyone had their eye on loot: "As for the business of pillage, there is nothing that more bewitcheth them, nor anything wherein they promise themselves so loudly, nor delight in more mainly", and one Spaniard wrote to his family: "Pray to God for me that he will grant me in England the house of some rich merchant . . . and he will ransom it from me for 30,000 ducats".

Fire from the ship's galley and from gunpowder was a constant fear on both English and Spanish ships, since they were so combustible. English orders of 1568 required

. . . that no Captain suffer any beds of straw within the ship, for it is perilous for firework: and the said Captain to cause two hogsheads [barrels] to be cut asunder in the midst and chained to the side; the soldiers and mariners to piss into that they may always be full of urine to quench fire with and two or three pieces of old sail ready to wet in the piss. (*Orders to Be Used in the King's or Queen's Majesties' Ships*, 1568)

The need for good discipline was greater on Armada ships than on English vessels, because there were so many soldiers on board:

It is of the greatest importance to the success of the Armada that there should exist perfect good feeling and friendship between soldiers and sailors, and that there should be no possibility of quarrels amongst them. . . . I therefore order that no man shall carry a dagger.

Medina Sidonia knew very well how troops behaved unless controlled:

The soldiers must allow the rations to be distributed by those appointed for the duty, and must not themselves go down and take or choose them by force, as they have sometimes done.

The greatest problem was the victualling and good health of the enormous number of men involved. No one had ever administered such a difficult undertaking before. Salted meat and water (or beer) stored in barrels tended to go putrid. Every delay in putting to sea made food spoilage more likely. A few days out of Lisbon the Spanish reported: "We have had to throw a large part of the food overboard

45 Title page of the *Mariners Mirrour*, the first English-language edition of Wagenhaer's charts and navigational directions for Europe, 1588. It was the most important navigational publication of the century. Note the navigational instruments and the garb of the mariners (who are "weighing the lead" to test the depth of water).

on the days that biscuit is not served out. . . . On Sundays and Thursdays every man will receive six ounces bacon and two ounces rice. On Mondays and Wednesdays six ounces of cheese and three ounces of beans or chick peas. . . the ordinary water ration must not exceed three pints a day for all purposes.

The English *Memorandum as to Victualling* laid down the ration on a 28-day month basis, of which 10 were fish days and 16 flesh days (two fish days were "saved" ingeniously because on Fridays only half rations were issued).

The fare of fish days for every man per diem biscuit one pound, one quarter of stockfish, or an eighth part of a ling, one quarter of a pound of cheese, half a quarter in butter, one gallon of beer.

The flesh day beer and biscuit as above, flesh two pounds salf beef per diem, so as every man hath one pound for a meal, and four men have four pounds for a meal. For one day in the week one pound of bacon for a man per diem, a pint of pease for one man for a meal.

Reality seldom matched theory. During Drake's campaign against Cadiz, one ship's crew mutinied, petitioning their captain:

46 An artist's impression of Drake and his crew on the quarter deck.

because it was only giving men the plague and making them sick." On both sides, the victuallers proved venal and careless.

The English fleet, having been reduced to half strength during the winter months of 1587-8, was in better shape than the Armada, where men had been living in ships for months. The official ration laid down for each fleet indicates that, despite the fact that crews seldom received the full ration, the English fleet was better fed than the Armada.

Spanish Ration Allocation:
Each man to receive one and a half pounds of biscuits per day, or two pounds of fresh bread

Our allowance is so small we are not able to live any longer on it. . . . For what is a piece of beef of half a pound among four men to dinner . . . [and] a little beverage worse than pump water . . . you make no men of us, but beasts.

During the Armada campaign itself Howard warned Burghley:

We have scarcely three weeks' victuals left in our fleet . . . there is here the gallantest company of captains, soldiers, and mariners that I think ever was seen in England. It were a pity they should lack meat, when they are so desirous to spend their lives in her Majesty's service.

As the months slipped by, Howard commented:

We think it should be marvelled at how we keep our men from running away, for the worst men in the fleet knoweth for how long we are victualled;

but I thank God as yet we are not troubled with any mutinies, nor I hope shall not, for I see men kindly handled will bear want and run through fire and water.

Howard's surviving correspondence during the Armada campaign is dominated by the victualling problem and ill health. When not on duty the men lived below deck, in the foetid semi-darkness. They slept on the wooden deck, although in 1587 Hawkins introduced the hammock into the navy. He had seen it used in the West Indies. There were no latrines, only buckets, and seasickness and diarrhoea were endemic. Decks were washed down into the bilges, the filth often polluting the food stored above the ballast. No wonder sickness was the greatest danger:

God of his mercy keep us from the sickness, for we fear that more than any hurt that the Spaniards will do. . . . We must now man ourselves again, for we cast many overboard, and a number in great extremity which we discharged. I have sent with all expedition

47 A colourful version of the attack by fireships illustrates the way in which the event was greatly elaborated and exaggerated afterwards.

[haste] a priest for more men.

Only two days before the Armada was sighted off the English coast, Howard reported:

Some four or five ships have discharged their men for the sickness in some is great, so that we are fain to discharge some ships, to have their men to furnish the others.

During the chase up the North Sea one captain gave up the pursuit for lack of powder and meat, his men so desperate for water that they were drinking their own urine. The main killers were gastro-enteritis, typhoid and scurvy. One contemporary described the symptoms of scurvy:

The sailors fall with sundry diseases, their gums wax great and swell, so that they are fain to cut them away, their legs swell, and all the body becometh sore, and so benummed that they cannot stirre hand nor foot. (Richard Hakluyt, *The Principal Voyages, Traffiques and Discoveries of the English Nation*, 1598-1602)

Ordinary mariners tell us nothing of what battle was like, although everyone agrees that the battle off Gravelines was hot. Pedro Coco Calderon, purser of one of the ships that returned safely to Spain, wrote:

The enemy [the English fleet] then opened a heavy artillery fire on our flagship at seven o'clock in the morning, which was continued for nine hours. So tremendous was the fire that over 200 balls struck the sails and hull of the flagship on the starboard side, killing and wounding many men, disabling and dismounting three guns, and destroying much rigging. The holes made in the hull between wind and water caused so great leakage that two divers had as much as they could do to stop them up with tow [flax] and lead plates, working all day. The crew were much exhausted by nightfall with their heavy labours at the guns, without food."

But fewer than 2000 of the Armada's estimated 20,000 casualties died in battle, and less than 200 on the English side. Ten times as many died of sickness.

VICTIMS AND SURVIVORS

When the two fleets returned home, the scene of desolation was great. Howard was deeply shocked:

Sickness and mortality begins wonderfully to grow amongst us; and it is a most pitiful sight to see, here at Margate, how men, having no place to receive them into here, die in the streets. I am

driven myself, of force, to come a-land, to see them bestowed in some lodging; and the best I can get is barns and such outhouse; and the relief is small that I can provide for them here. It would grieve a man's heart to see them that have served so valiantly to die so miserably.

Medina Sidonia had a similar picture to report:

On board some of the ships that are in there has not been a drop of water to drink for a fortnight. On my own ship, a hundred and eighty men have died of sickness, three out of the four pilots succombed, and all the rest of the people on board are ill, many of typhus and other infectious diseases. All the sixty men of my own household have either died or fallen sick, and only two remain able to serve me . . . we are now worse off than ever, for the men are all ill and the little biscuit and wine we have left will be finished in a week. We are therefore in a wretched state, and I implore your Majesty to send some money quickly to buy necessities. . . . Everything is in disorder, and must at once be put in competent hands, for I am in no condition to attend business.

The fate of the *Elizabeth Jonas*, an unusually unlucky ship, indicates the proportions the problem of epidemic could take:

The Elizabeth Jonas . . . hath had a great infection in her from the beginning, so as of the 500 men which she carried out, by the time we had been in Plymouth three weeks or a month, there were dead of them 200 and above; so as I was driven to set all the rest of her men ashore, to take out her ballast, and to make fires in her of wet broom . . . and so hoped thereby to have cleansed her of her infection; and thereupon got new men, very tall and able as ever I saw. . . .

48 A chart of the Armada's course around the British Isles.

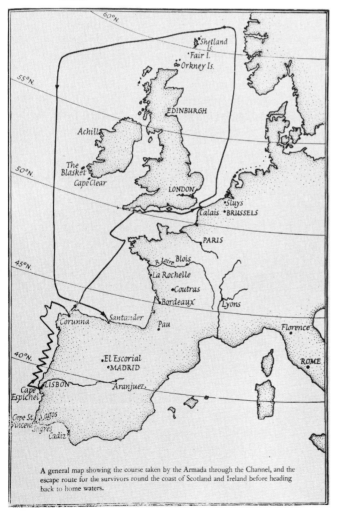

A general map showing the course taken by the Armada through the Channel, and the escape route for the survivors round the coast of Scotland and Ireland before heading back to home waters.

Now the infection is broken out in greater extremity than ever it did before, and the men die and sicken faster than ever they did.

In both countries the local population watched almost with indifference as sailors and soldiers died in the streets. These were hard times, though not altogether heartless. In England, in addition to their modest wages, a bonus was awarded to those who had manned the fireships at Calais, to the severely wounded men, and to the surviving sick of the

Elizabeth Jonas. Two years later Hawkins and Drake took the lead in establishing the "Chatham Chest", a fund for the relief of sick and aged mariners.

The Armada's journey home was a far greater nightmare than anyone could have imagined. Medina Sidonia had put the whole fleet on half rations and issued strict orders for the long journey around the British Isles:

You will take great care not to be driven on the coast of Ireland, for fear of the harm that may come to you there. Leaving the islands and rounding the cape in 61 ½° [the northern point of Shetland], you will run west south west until you reach 58°, then south west to the height of 53°, and then south south west, heading for Cape Finisterre, so find your way to Corunna or Ferol, or any other port in the coast of Galicia.

However, the ships encountered worse weather than most had ever experienced, and shortly after passing Cape Wrath on about 21 August the Armada dispersed in heavy seas. At least 26 ships foundered on the Irish coast, though it is not clear whether they were all driven ashore unwillingly, since the crews were exhausted and half crazed for lack of water.

The experiences of most of those shipwrecked were truly awful. The most fortunate were the 300 crew of the cargo ship *Gran Grifon*, one of whom wrote:

Truly our one thought was that our lives were ended, and each of us reconciled himself to God as well as he could, and prepared for the long journey of death. To force the ship any more would only have ended it and our lives the sooner, so we gave up trying. The poor soldiers too, who had worked incessantly at the pumps and buckets, lost heart and let the water rise. . . . At last when we thought all hope was gone . . . we sighted an island ahead of us. It was Fair Isle, and we anchored in a sheltered spot we found.

The *Gran Grifon* was broken to pieces by the waves, but all got ashore. It was mid-November before they were rescued by the Scots and taken to the mainland of Scotland, by which time they had eaten all the livestock on the island. Another eight months were spent waiting in Edinburgh, before the crew was shipped to France, and thence home, in the summer of 1589. No other shipwrecks had such a happy ending.

50 A Spanish ship founders on the Irish coast.

Juan de Nova

Juan de Nova was either the servant or companion of Don Alonso de Luzon, captain of the *Trinidad Valancera*. It is not known what became of Juan de Nova but he wrote a vivid account of the crew's journey home. The *Trinidad Valencera* ran aground on a reef in Donegal. Four hundred and fifty men were brought ashore before the ship broke up; the rest of the crew was drowned. Don Alonso led his men towards a castle held by a Catholic bishop, which he hoped to occupy. However, on the way they were confronted by an English force of 200 cavalry and a similar number of infantry. The Spanish were told

... they must surrender as prisoners of war. They replied that if that was the only alternative, they would rather die fighting, as befitted Spaniards.

The English answered that if they did not surrender at once, 3,000 of the Queen's troops would come shortly and cut all their throats. They still persisted in their refusal to surrender, and they remained halted all that night. The next night the enemy sounded the attack at two or three points, and a skirmish commenced, which continued the whole night.

The next morning, whilst they were endeavouring to better their position, they heard

51 Part of the awesome Irish coastline with which the Armada had to contend.

the enemy's drums sound again for a parley. . . . The major made them many offers and promises if they would surrender, and in view of this and that his men were dying of hunger and that the enemy had cut off all supplies, the colonel [Don Alonso] replied that he could lay down his arms on fair terms of war, if they would keep their

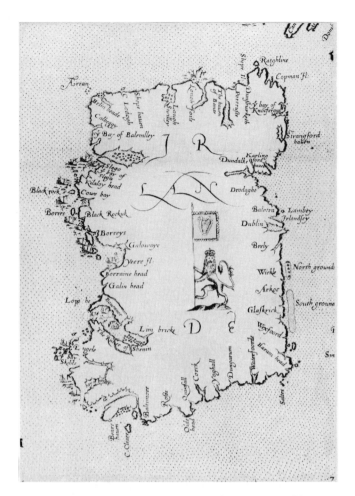

52 A contemporary map of Ireland, marking 16 known shipwrecks; since then, a total of 26 sites have been identified.

53 A modern map, marking 24 of the 26 sites (© George Philip and Son Ltd). Asterisks indicate tentatively identified marks. Compare this with the previous, contemporary map and you will see one reason for disaster – the Armada was unaware of how far west the coastline of Co. Mayo and Galway lay.

promise, and allow each man to retain the best suit of clothes he had. They gave their word that this should be done, and the Spaniards lay down their arms. As soon as the enemy had possession of them, and had conveyed them to the other side of the bog towards Dublin, they fell upon the Spaniards in a body and despoiled them of everthing they possessed, leaving them quite naked, and killing those who offered the least resistance.

The next morning, at daybreak, the enemy came to separate some other officers who were amongst the soldiers, and put them inside a square with the rest. The remaining soldiers were then made to go into an open field, and a line of the enemy's harquebussiers [men armed with a harquebus, a portable gun] approached them on the one side and a body of cavalry on the other, killing over 300 of them with lance and bullet.

Juan de Nova reported that 150 escaped this massacre, but that their numbers steadily dwindled as they were passed from one friendly Irish chief to another, and then shipped to Scotland. Eventually, James VI sent the survivors, now barely 40 in number, in four ships to France to be repatriated. Storms forced the ships twice to shelter in English ports where the crews were ordered to hand over the Spaniards. James VI, however, had commanded the crews not to abandon them, and they refused to yield. The Spaniards eventually reached France and made their way home overland.

The officers were marched naked or semi-naked to Drogheda. Some died on the way from exhaustion, and the rest were interrogated. Only Don Alonso and one other officer survived.

Christopher Carleill (1551-93)

The barbarity of the English can be explained partly by fear. The garrison in Ireland was only 2000 strong. As the first reports of Spanish landings were received it was unclear whether they had come as castaways or invaders. With so few men available, and possibly nervous, having himself arrived in Ireland only three weeks earlier, the Lord Deputy instructed that all Spanish captives should be executed.

Captain Christopher Carleill had been appointed as Constable of Carrickfergus in Co. Antrim that summer and was then promoted to Governor of Ulster. No doubt he shared the apprehensions of others who feared there might be a popular Irish rising against the English: "God be thanked the people of these remote parts stirred not, but made to the sea coast being, as it seemed, more greedy of spoil than apt to hearken to other things". As the Lord Deputy reported, "The country people, having stripped the Spaniards of their rich apparel and robbed them of a great store of money, chains and jewels, turned them loose. . . ."

As the days went by, and it became clear that the Spanish had nothing else in mind but refuge, some junior officers protested against the Lord Deputy's savagery. Christopher Carleill was one of them.

Into the hands of this man there fell fourteen Spaniards who had saved themselves from their wrecked ship, and who gave themselves up to him begging that as a soldier he should spare

54 Christopher Carleill.

their lives. It seemed to him that he should use military pity, and therefore he received them chivalrously without cruelty or grudging. But having some commission to carry out, he sent them to Sir William Fitzwilliam, the Lord Deputy, writing about their case, paying out money for their expenses and recommending to him that he should honour the promises made to them. But this did not help these poor wretches in the least, for the Lord Deputy was sour of soul and severe . . . and sent them back to Captain Carleill with orders that he should put them to death in any manner – meaning on the gallows, as was done to other similar survivors by other persons. Nevertheless, Captain Carleill, being a gentleman by nature and an experienced soldier, careful of his honour and not wanting to sully his hands with the blood of those poor people, put everthing to the decision of the elements (it not being possible for him to do any more) and relying on the promises of a few Scottish boatmen, he embarked them on a small ship of theirs, which by chance was in those parts, gave them money to get rid of them; sending them to Scotland. . . . (Petruccio Ubaldino [a Protestant Italian, living in London], *The Spanish Armada*, 1589)

Carleill, of course, was guilty of gross disobedience and insubordination. He was no stranger to blood-letting, nor to the cheapness of life, but one must assume that besides his own integrity in this matter his self-confidence stemmed from an illustrious military record in the Netherlands and with Drake in the West Indies. He was also Walsingham's son-in-law, and must have known he stood a good chance of avoiding punishment. If there was an open quarrel with Fitzwilliam it seems to have been

55 Sir William Fitzwilliam, the ruthless Lord Deputy of Ireland.

made up. But Carleill's career petered out, and he spent his last years in penury.

Captain Francisco de Cuellar

On 4 October 1589 Captain Francisco de Cuellar sat down in a room in Antwerp and wrote a remarkable letter to an unnamed friend in Spain: "You will be astonished at seeing this letter on account of the slight certainty that could have existed as to my being alive. . . ."

On 10 August 1588 de Cuellar had been condemned to hang for letting his ship break formation, sailing ahead of the Armada. He managed to talk himself out of punishment, though another captain condemned at the same time was less fortunate. De Cuellar's ship was one of three driven ashore in Donegal Bay, where they began to break up in the surf. Unable to swim,

I placed myself on the poop of my ship. . . . Many were drowning in the ships, others, casting themselves into the water, sank to the bottom without returning to the surface; others on rafts and barrels . . . the waves swept others aways, washing them out of the ships . . . when any one of our people reached the beach two hundred savages and other enemies fell upon him and stripped him of what he had on until he was left in his naked skin.

De Cuellar floated ashore on a hatch cover, his legs having been crushed by a piece of timber in the sea. He crawled up on to the beach.

The enemies and savages, who were on the beach stripping those who had been able to reach it by swimming, did not touch me, seeing me . . . with my legs and hands and my linen trousers covered with blood.

De Cuellar hid in some rushes with another man.

I turned to call my companion . . . and found he was dead. . . . There he lay on the ground with more than six hundred other dead bodies which the sea cast up. . . . At dawn I began to walk, little by little, searching for a monastery . . . and I arrived with much trouble and toil. I found it deserted and the church and images of the saints burned and completely ruined, and twelve Spaniards hanging within the church. . . . I decided to go to the shore where the ships lay. . . . I saw two poor Spanish soldiers approaching, stripped naked as when they were born, crying out and calling upon God to help them. . . . I entered a wood where an old savage of more than seventy years came out from behind the rocks, and two young men with their arms – one English . . . and a girl of the age of twenty years most beautiful. . . . The Englishman came up, saying "Yield Spanish poltroon," and made a slash at me with a knife. . . . I warded off the blow with a stick I carried in my hand but in the end he got me and cut the sinew of my right leg. He went to repeat the blow immediately, had not the savage come up with his daughter, who may have been his mistress. They took him away from me, and the savage began to strip me, to

56 A figurehead, showing Philip's arms; from the Spanish ship wrecked at Streedagh, near Sligo, which could well be de Cuellar's ship.

the taking off of my shirt under which I wore a gold chain. . . . When they saw it, they rejoiced greatly. . . . The girl lamented much to see the bad treatment I received and asked them to leave me the clothes and not to injure me any more. I remained in the trees, bleeding from the wound. . . . From the hut they sent me a boy with a poultice made of herbs to put on my wound, and butter and milk and a small piece of oaten bread to eat.

De Cuellar was directed to some huts where he was given shelter that night. The following morning he was given a horse and a boy to show him the way. When over 150 English horsemen rode by they hid behind rocks, but then he fell in with

. . . more than forty savages on foot, and they wished to make little pieces of me because they were all Lutherans [*i.e. Protestants*]. They did not, as the boy who came with me told them that his master had taken me prisoner and that he had me in custody.

Eventually, de Cuellar made his way to a friendly village, where they found 70 more Spaniards and learnt of a Spanish ship on the coast. Because of his injuries de Cuellar failed to reach the ship. He was lucky, for as it sailed it ran aground and was smashed to pieces on the rocks. Those of the ship's company who were not drowned were killed by English troops on the beach. Once more, de Cuellar seemed to be sole survivor.

A priest helped him reach the island fortress (in Lough Melvin) held by Dartry MacClancy.

They helped me as best they could with a blanket to wear of the kind they use and remained three months, acting as a real savage like themselves. The wife of the chieftain was beautiful in the extreme, and showed me much kindness.

De Cuellar had a chance to reflect on his circumstances and those of his hosts:

These savages liked us well because they knew we came against the heretics [i.e. the English Protestants] and were such great enemies of theirs, and if it had not been for those who guarded us as their own persons, not one of us would have been left alive. We had goodwill to them for this, although they were the first to rob us and strip to the skin those who came alive to land.

When English troops approached, MacClancy fled to the hills, while de Cuellar, with eight other Spaniards who had also been under MacClancy's protection, successfully defended the fortress against the 1800-strong

English force, who abandoned their seige when snow started to fall. MacClancy treated de Cuellar as a hero, but this had its own dangers:

To me he offered to give a sister of his in marriage. I thanked him much for this but contented myself with a guide to direct me to a place where I could meet with a ship for Scotland. He did not wish to give me permission [to leave], nor to any Spaniard of those who were with him . . . his sole object was to detain us, that we might act as his guard.

Eventually, de Cuellar and four of the other Spaniards managed to escape under cover of night, and 20 days later they arrived at the Giant's Causeway.

One day I heard of . . . where there were some vessels that were going to Scotland. Thither I travelled, crawling along, for I could scarcely move because of a wound in one leg; but, as it led to safety, I did all I could to walk and reach it quickly. The vessels had left two days before. . . . I did not know what to do, as the

57 The gold cross of a Knight of Malta, belonging to the captain of the *Girona* a galleass which sank near the Giant's Causeway, Co. Antrim; the ship was recovered in 1968.

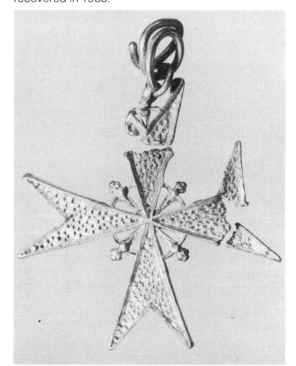

soldiers who came with me had left and gone to another port further on to seek for a passage. . . . Some women when they saw me alone and ill, pitied me, and took me away to their little huts in the mountain and kept me there for more than a month and a half in safety and cured me.

As luck would have it, some English soldiers came to the hut. Because of de Cuellar's bad leg they decided to get a horse to carry him to Dublin.

I told him I was very willing to do whatever they wished, and to go with them, with which they were reassured, and began to make fun with the girls. Their mother made signs to me to get out, and I did so in great haste, leaping banks as I went along.

Two days later, the English were still searching for him, but with local help de Cuellar at last got a ship to Scotland. Once again, he experienced the terror of rough seas and contrary winds. De Cuellar was deeply disappointed by James VI, "for he did no good to anyone". After further privations, he at last boarded one of four boats heading for Dunkirk in the Spanish Netherlands. Elizabeth had undertaken not to molest these ships, but

All was treacherous; for an agreement had been made with the ships of Holland that they should put to sea and await us . . . and there put us all to death, without sparing anyone. The Dutch did as they were commanded. . . . God willed that of the four vessels in which we came two escaped and grounded, where they went to pieces. . . . They could not come to our assistance with the boats from the port of Dunkirk, as the enemy cannonaded them briskly. . . . The sea and wind were very high so that we were in the greatest peril of being all lost. However we cast ourselves afloat on timbers, and some soldiers drowned. . . . I reached shore in my shirt without any other clothing. It was sad to see us enter the town once more, stripped naked, and for the other part we saw before our eyes the Dutch making a thousand pieces of 270 Spaniards who came in the ship which brought us . . . leaving not more than three alive.

It is difficult to imagine that Francisco de Cuellar, sea captain though he was, ever went near a ship again.

AFTERWORD

It is worth speculating on what might have happened if the Armada had successfully landed Parma's troops in Kent. It is unlikely that the English army could have withstood them, but could they have brought the whole of England to submission? What was abundantly clear was that the English Catholics had little heart for Spanish rule over England. Moreover, Philip himself, as the sealed letter Medina Sidonia was to hand to Parma indicated, was willing to settle for three conditions:

The first is that in England the free use and exercise of our holy Catholic faith shall be permitted to all Catholics, native and foreign, and that those who are in exile shall be allowed to return. The second is that all the places in my Netherlands which the English hold shall be restored to me; and the third that the English shall compensate me for the injury they have done me, my dominions and subjects.

The last condition was a bargaining point. It is difficult to believe that Parma would have been anything other than speechless with anger had he opened this letter, since he could have achieved an English withdrawal from the Netherlands by parley, as he had wanted to do, and he was far too pragmatic a man to invade England purely to achieve religious toleration.

However, if submission had been achieved it is possible that England would have become a satellite of Catholic Spain. In that case the Dutch revolt would probably have been finally crushed, and Philip might even have intervened more directly in French politics to end the hopes of the Huguenots.

58 An Armada commemorative medal, with the Latin *"Flavit et dissipati sunt"*, "He [God] breathed, and they were scattered".

Protestantism would have been banished to the fringes of European affairs.

The defeat of the Spanish Armada has always been held in England to have been decisive. It is understandable that Englishmen at the time thought so. However, far from suffering a decisive reverse, Spain's seapower increased during the last decade of the century, and the English navy found it far harder to attack Spanish shipping. More gold and silver reached Spain during that final decade than had ever done previously. Before the Armada, Hawkins and Drake had advocated the blockade of Spain's coastline, and they could probably have come close to achieving this. After 1588, this was no longer feasible, because of Spain's increased naval power, and England's attacks, notably in 1589, were dismal failures. It could also be said that the economic difficulties which the Stuarts inherited were partly the legacy of the Spanish war, which only came to an end when Elizabeth died.

Yet, in two vital respects the Armada episode was decisive. In matters of naval warfare, the clash of these two great fleets established beyond all doubt the supremacy of gun and sail over the galley and hand-to-hand melée which had characterized most battles at sea hitherto. This, more than Lepanto, decided the future outcome of the struggle between Christian and Muslim in the Mediterranean.

In the political sphere, all Europe had awaited the outcome of the Armada expedition with bated breath, for the religious on both sides saw in it God's judgment. For the Protestants, and indeed for the Catholic states uneasy with Spain, England's victory was greeted with relief and rejoicing. While Spain remained unquestionably the first power in Europe for another generation, that power was now seen to be limited, and the danger of Europe becoming a single religious unit again had passed.

Finally, the Armada experience was a personal watershed for many of the leading participants. For Elizabeth herself, of course, it thrust her yet higher in popular esteem. But for English commanders it was a glory from which there could only be descent. Not one of the main participants, Howard, Drake, Frobisher or Hawkins, ever enjoyed the same degree of public adulation again. On the Spanish side, Medina Sidonia's career was destroyed, and he retreated from public affairs for the rest of his life. Philip, alone, refused to allow defeat to change him. He plodded on with one scheme after another to bring down his adversary Elizabeth until relieved by death in 1598.

DATE LIST

(All dates are in the new style. England continued to use old-style dates, ten days behind the new style, until the eighteenth century.)

1554 Philip marries Mary Tudor to forge Anglo-Spanish alliance.

1555 Philip becomes ruler of the Netherlands.

1556 Philip becomes King of Spain on his father, Charles V's, abdication.

1558 Elizabeth becomes Queen of England.

1562 Commencement of Catholic-Huguenot struggle in France.

1568 Beginning of the Dutch armed revolt. Mary Stuart flees to England, where she is kept under house arrest. Hawkins and Drake ambushed by Spanish at San Juan de Ulloa – heralds the beginning of English privateering against Spain. Money for the Spanish Netherlands' army "borrowed" by Elizabeth when carriers put in to English ports.

1570 Papal edict denouncing Elizabeth as a heretic.

1571 The Duke of Alva, in the Netherlands, offers to invade England for Philip. Naval battle of Lepanto – Turks defeated by Spanish under Don John of Austria and Santa Cruz.

1572 The massacre of Bartholemew's Day in Paris – 10,000 Huguenots die.

1577 Drake circumnavigates the world, returning in 1580 with plunder from Spanish ships. Hawkins appointed Treasurer of the Navy Board and begins reforms.

1580 Philip invades Portugal and seizes the throne.

1582 Santa Cruz defeats Strozzi's fleet off the Azores.

1583 Santa Cruz first offers to defeat the English navy and invade England.

1584 Throckmorton Plot uncovered – Ambassador Mendoza expelled from England. Assassination of William of Orange.

1585 Spain recaptures Antwerp. Treaty of Nonsuch, whereby England pledges financial and military support to the Dutch rebels.

1586 Philip instructs Santa Cruz to estimate the Armada requirement. He reduces Santa Cruz's estimate, seeks estimate from Parma and finally combines the two plans. Mary Stuart disinherits her son, James VI, and nominates Philip as her successor as heir to the English throne. Babington Plot uncovered.

1587

February Mary Stuart executed.

April–June Drake attacks Cadiz, and other Spanish targets, delaying the Armada preparations by a fatal eight weeks and making it impossible to sail before autumn equinox.

August Parma captures Sluys, an essential port for the invasion.

September Parma completes assembly of his army for the planned arrival of the Armada. As a feint, he also offers to negotiate a peace with England.

October Santa Cruz persuades Philip to delay the sailing of the Armada.

December Philip urges Santa Cruz to sail as soon as possible. The English fleet is put on full alert, fearing the Armada is about to sail.

1588

January The English fleet is reduced to half strength as intelligence indicates the Armada is unlikely to sail before March or April.

February Santa Cruz dies, and Philip appoints Medina Sidonia in his place. Parma's offer of peace negotiations is responded to by Elizabeth, who sends peace commissioners to the Netherlands.

May 30 Armada sets sail but runs into adverse weather.

June 2 Howard's fleet joins Drake's at Plymouth.

June 19 The Armada reaches Corunna, where it has to refit.

July 17 The English fleet attempts to find Armada off Spain but is turned back by adverse winds.

July 22 The Armada sets sail again. The English fleet returns to Plymouth.

July 29 The Armada is seen off the Lizard.

	That night the English fleet sails out of Plymouth Sound.
July 30	The Armada sails slowly up the Channel, the English fleet sails westward to meet the Armada. On the night of the 30 July the English fleet manages to get to the western, windward, side of the Armada (the wind is blowing from the S.W.).
July 31	First battle, between Eddystone and Start Point. In the night, Drake captures the galleon *Rosario*.
August 1	The galleon *San Salvador* accidentally blows up and begins to sink. English capture her and tow her to Weymouth to be salvaged.
August 2	Battle of Portland Bill – both sides expend much ammunition.
August 6	Armada reaches Calais Roads and anchors. English fleet anchors to the west, just beyond artillery range.
August 7	Howard sends to England for expendable fireships to break up Armada before Parma can come out to sea. Medina Sidonia learns for the first time that Parma is in Bruges, not on the coast, and that he will not be ready for another six days. Howard decides he cannot afford to wait for fireships from England and selects eight ships from his own fleet, which are sent into Armada after tide turns at about 11 p.m. Armada cuts cables
	and scatters to avoid fireships.
August 8	The English fleet attacks Armada galleons off Gravelines and decisively defeats them, sinking four ships. The rest of the Armada is drifting easwards towards Netherlands sandbanks.
August 9	Armada spends morning desperately trying to avoid the sandbanks, with a strong NNW wind blowing. Just after midday wind changes and Armada escapes northwards.
August 11	The English fleet decides to pursue the Armada northwards until the Firth of Forth.
August 12	Medina Sidonia and his commanders decide finally that returning to the English Channel is out of the question. Medina Sidonia gives orders for the return journey around British Isles.
August 18	Elizabeth reviews her troops at Tilbury.
August 21	The Armada passes Cape Wrath but begins to break up and disperse in heavy seas.
September 23	Medina Sidonia's ship reaches Spain; other ships drift in over the next three or four weeks.
1589	Drake and Norris attack Portugal but mission fails.
1596	Drake dies at sea of dysentery.
1598	Philip II dies.
1603	Elizabeth I dies.
1604	James I (and VI) ends war with Spain.

BIOGRAPHICAL NOTES

William Allen (1532-94). Leader of the English Catholics in exile and the main propagandist for Philip's claim to the English Crown. He founded the English College in Douai with the specific purpose of training a body of English Catholics to re-establish the Catholic faith. His political career began in 1582. He was in contact with Mary Stuart, and knew of the plans to overthrow Elizabeth. Once it was clear James VI would not embrace Catholicism Allen became leader of "the Spanish party" among English Catholics. When Philip prepared his invasion plans he persuaded Pope Sixtus V to create Allen a Cardinal, to be installed at Canterbury when the invasion took place. The appointment was quickly understood in Rome, where Sixtus V reported to Philip "Throughout all Rome there arose forthwith a universal cry – now they are getting things into order for a war with England."

Pedro Menendez de Aviles (1519-74). The finest sailor Spain produced in the sixteenth century. It was Philip's misfortune that he died before putting his plans against the English into practice. He alone saw that the privateers sailing to the Caribbean could only be defeated in the English Channel. Philip was persuaded, and in 1574 Menendez started to assemble a large fleet to support the Netherlands' army and to control the English Channel. His key plan was the seizure of the Scilly Isles as a permanent base for a fleet of ships which could patrol the length of the Channel. Had he succeeded, the war between England and Spain would have been dramatically different. But he and many others died in a violent epidemic which swept through the fleet in 1574. No one else followed Menedez' lead, and with him died Philip's best hope of defeating England at sea.

Robert Dudley, Earl of Leicester (1532-88). Might well have married Elizabeth if he had not already married Amy Robsart. Despite brief quarrels Elizabeth remained deeply fond of him all her life. He, even more than Walsingham, forced Elizabeth into more open hostility with

Spain and destroyed Burghley's peace policy. His command of the Netherlands expedition, 1586-7 was a disaster, since he quarrelled with the Dutch leaders and with his own subordinates, while achieving no military success of any note. Nevertheless, Elizabeth appointed him Captain General of the 10,000-strong land forces during the Armada campaign. He assembled these at Tilbury, on the north bank of the Thames, a poor choice in view of the fact that Philip planned the Spanish landing to take place at Margate. Leicester died a month later, to Elizabeth's great distress.

Sir Martin Frobisher (1535?-94). Best known for his repeated attempts to find the "north-west passage" to Cathay. During the Armada campaign Frobisher commanded a division, and was knighted by Howard for his services. He seems to have been jealous of Drake and his seizure of the valuable *Rosario* (see page 45): "He thinketh to cozen us of our shares of 15,000 ducats, but we will have our shares, or I will make him spend the best blood in his belly." With characteristic resentment but scant understanding of Drake's tactical skill, Frobisher accused him of cowardice at Gravelines: "He came bragging up at first indeed, and gave them his prow and his broadside; and then kept his luff and was glad he was gone again like a cowardly knave." He died of a wound sustained fighting the Spanish near Brest.

Don Juan de Idiaquez (? – 1614). One of Philip's closest advisers in Madrid. His father had been secretary and political adviser to Charles V. Idiaquez was secretary to both Philip II and Philip III. He had responsibility for foreign affairs in Philip's informal cabinet, the Junta de Noche (the Committee of the Night). Each day Idiaquez would receive papers from his foreign affairs council, to which he would add a précis and recommendation in the margin, for the King's consideration. Usually the King would instruct his secretary how to reply, or draft a response himself. Much of the correspondence

ROBERT DUDLEY Erle
of Leicester, lo de Steward of
howshold to Queene Elizabeth,
for his singuler gyfts of the
mynde & graces of his person
was aduaunced, honored, and
followed more then others.
He dyed the 55 yeare of his
age, Anno 1588.

59 Leicester, Elizabeth's favourite for 40 years.

sent to Mendoza, Parma and to Santa Cruz and Medina Sidonia was drafted and signed by Idiaquez, though one is always conscious of Philip's close watch on everything despatched or received.

James VI (1566-1625). Came to the Scottish throne on his mother's enforced abdication in 1567. During his minority he was the victim of struggles between different cliques of nobles, which, broadly speaking, favoured alliance either with England or with France. James had to balance the need for friendship with England (to inherit its crown on Elizabeth's death), against his need to escape the clutches of pro-English nobles who had held him once as a captive. As the European crisis grew it proved increasingly difficult to steer a middle path. In 1586 he signed a treaty with England. His mother had already disinherited him in favour of Philip. When Mary was condemned to death Elizabeth made sure James knew about it. He could not afford to burn his boats completely with the Catholic faction, but while "it cannot stand with his honour to be a consenter to take his mother's life" Elizabeth correctly inferred that he would not interfere in the event of execution. In the meantime, he allowed Scottish Catholics to co-operate with Philip II. James left his options open in case things went against the Protestant cause, even arranging the repatriation of some shipwrecked Spaniards. The English knew this well enough, but his skilful handling of this situation did not prejudice his inheritance of the English throne.

Don Alonso Martinez de Leyva (? – 1588). Made his reputation in the war against the Moors in Granada, and then in the Netherlands. When Philip grew impatient with Santa Cruz it was de Leyva, whose knowledge of seafaring was slight, whom he sent to chivvy him in May 1587. When the Armada eventually set sail, de Leyva had command of the vanguard of the Armada, on the starboard flank, and was to take command of the troops in the event of a landing in England separately from Parma's army. De Leyva conducted himself with distinction, particularly in the battle of Gravelines on 8 August. But his ship ran aground on the Irish coast. He made two attempts to escape to Scotland on other grounded ships, the second being the galleass *Girona*. But off northern Ireland the *Girona* ran into a northerly gale

60 Mendoza expelled from England, 1584, carries, symbolically, details of English ports in his left hand, and a list of English Catholic gentry in his right hand. On the left, a conspirator, possibly Throckmorton, is punished.

The Spanish Embassad: thrust out of England.

which blew her on to a reef off Lacada Point, Co. Antrim, not far from the Giant's Causeway. De Leyva and all the ship's company, save five, were drowned.

Bernadino de Mendoza (1540-1604). Spain's ambassador in London, but expelled in 1584 for complicity in the Throckmorton plot. He was transferred to Paris, carrying with him a deep hatred of Protestant England. He constructed a highly effective spy network among English Catholics and others. He was the first man in Paris to learn of Mary Stuart's execution. He was probably the best informed diplomat in all Europe, but with a fatal aptitude to believe what he wanted to hear, for example that the English Catholics would rise in rebellion. He sat at the hub of a wheel of intrigue, between Philip II in Madrid, Parma in the Netherlands, and Olivares, the Spanish ambassador in Rome. His most important task was to ensure France would be neutralized during the Armada expedition, a role which he carried out with skill. He financed the Duc de Guise against Henry III, and in May 1588 prompted the Duc into an attempted *coup d'etat*. Although it was bungled, Paris was sufficiently destabilized to guarantee French preoccupation with its own problems. His ability to believe what he wanted to hear was apparent when he refused to believe the Armada was defeated. As late as 29 September he wrote of the Armada refitting to resume its mission. By then Philip knew the truth very well, and noted in the margin of Mendoza's despatch: "Nothing of this is true. It will be well to tell him so." Mendoza returned to Madrid in 1591. His reputation never fully recovered from his miscalculation of the mood among English Catholics, or his optimistic reporting on the Armada's progress.

BOOK LIST

Collections of Documents

Almost all the quotations in this book have been taken from the following collections of documents, with the exception of those relating to particular individuals, which appear in the biographies listed below.

Richard Hakluyt, *The Principal Voyages, Traffiques and Discoveries of the English Nation* (numerous editions since first published 1598-1602)

Martin A.S. Hume, *Calendar of State Papers Relating to English Affairs*, Vol. IV, London, 1899 (consisting of translated Spanish correspondence)

J.K. Laughton, *State Papers Relating to The Defeat of the Spanish Armada*, Navy Records Soc., London, 1895 (2 vols., being mainly the English correspondence)

Stephen Usherwood, *The Great Enterprise, the History of the Spanish Armada*, London, 1978

Armada Books

Julian Corbett, *Drake and the Tudor Navy*, London, 1898

Niall Fallon, *The Armada in Ireland*, London, 1978

David Howarth, *The Voyage of the Arm. .da*, London, 1981

Alexander McKee, *From Merciless Invaders. An Eyewitness Account of the Spanish Armada*, London, 1963

Garrett Mattingly, *The Defeat of the Spanish Armada*, London, 1959

Armada Wrecks

Laurence Flanagan, *Girona*, Ulster Museum, 1974 (pamphlet on its collection from the wreck)

Colin Martin, *Full Fathom Five*, London, 1975

Robert Stenuit, *The Treasures of the Armada*, London, 1972

General Books on the Period, with an Emphasis on Seafaring

Carlo M. Cipolla, *Guns and Sails in the Early Phase of European Expansion, 1400-1700*, London, 1965

Peter Padfield, *Tide of Empires*, Vol 1: 1481-1654, London, 1979

A.L. Rowse, *The Expansion of Elizabethan England,* London, 1955

J. Williamson, *The Age of Drake*, London, 1938

J. Williamson, *The Tudor Age*, London, 1953

Books on Spain

R. Trevor Davies, *The Gold Century of Spain, 1501-1621*, London, 1937

Martin Hume, *Spain: Its Greatness and Decay, 1479-1788*, London, 1899

Geoffrey Parker, *The Army of Flanders*, Cambridge, 1972

Geoffrey Parker, *Spain and the Netherlands*, London, 1979

J.H. Parry, *The Spanish Seaborne Empire*, London, 1967

Individuals

Bryan Bevan, *The Great Seamen of Elizabeth I*, London, 1971

J.A. Froude, *English Seamen in the Sixteenth Century*, London, 1906

Elizabeth Jenkins, *Elizabeth the Great*, London, 1958

Christopher Lloyd, *Sir Francis Drake*, London, 1959

Rachel Lloyd, *Elizabethan Adventurer, The Life of Captain Christopher Carleill*, London, 1974

J.E. Neale, *Queen Elizabeth*, London, 1934

Geoffrey Parker, *Philip II*, London, 1979

Conyers Read, *Mr Secretary Walsingham*, London, 1925

Conyers Read, *Lord Burghley and Queen Elizabeth*, London, 1965

J.A. Williamson, *Sir Francis Drake*, London, 1951

J.A Williamson, *Hawkins of Plymouth*, London, 1949

Life as a Mariner

K. Andrews, *The Elizabethan Seaman: A Lecture*, National Maritime Museum, London, 1982

Christopher Lloyd, *The British Seaman*, London, 1968

Peter Kemp, *The British Sailor*, London, 1970

INDEX